THE *"WAR EFFORT"* GOT US OUT OF THE GREAT DEPRESSION!!

(the WPA etc. were but pittance employments)

WE NEED ANOTHER GOVERNMENT-GEARED MASS-TRANSFORMATION OF THE ECONOMY

This time, though, a *"peace-effort"*

Appleton Schneider

Millions of Americans are looking for work.

Prior to the election I'd first asked Mitt,
the prolific promiser . . .

WHAT JOBS ?

Contents

THE FALLACY OF FREE MARKET INDIVIDUALISM

In a brief chat with my boss, he opined that it's the sole fault of the "people" that we've come to this economic crisis. His retrospect is to a society of fiscal discipline, domestic responsibility, etc. People didn't buy what they couldn't afford . . . of course they didn't. There was no credit (= debt-collateral) back then.

This essay was my response to him.

PROVIDENTIAL PERSPECTIVE

FRICTION AND ENTROPY – OR FUSION AND SYNERGY?

A FEW PAGES OF FINAL CONSIDERATIONS

Regarding **Your** Oil . . .

What About the Middle East?

What about Netanyahu?

AN EMAIL FROM . . . . AND FROM ME BACK TO . . .

MITT !! *(I'd previously addressed . .)*

You gonna put between 15 and 23 million people to work on oil drilling, coal mining, and pipe fitting? No? Of course not. But, Mitt, what other jobs. All we've heard is promises, promises. Y'er gonna put America back to work.

DOING WHAT ???? *what jobs?????*
SPECIFY !!

So Mitt no longer matters. But the matter is Obama's to contend with, now for another four years. So far, during the last four, he hasn't been able to accomplish much.

Barack!!! What jobs???

Now it's up to you.

Maybe I can help?

You need to implement a Federally *mandated* and funded **"peace-mobilization"** based on the paradigm of the WW II "war-effort".

No, not ordering industrial conversion to weaponry manufacture.
Then to what?

I have a few suggestions here:

How about gray-water systems for sewage and such?
For men only, how about waterless urinals by law!?
(and for ultimate water-preservation . . . composting toilets for all??)
How about solar powered light through transparencies?
How wind/solar charged battery banks, providing at least the lighting and light-demand (tech. devices) power from a self-contained "grid" within a neighborhood or even single building?
How about timed traffic lights to keep the traffic moving, and cut the fuel consumption and pollution by absurd, sometimes enraging, sequential red-lights?
How about mandating installation of after-market engine shutoffs on all cars and trucks less than, perhaps, 6 years old? (Such systems are available on high-end cars now – not moving for x seconds and the engine shuts down, but just touch the gas pedal and it's up and running again instantly).
How about a battery-pack powered vehicle, (max. $3,000) bare-bones equipped for safety and comfort, just for commuting?? Might get 200mpg equivalent? No exhaust except from a mini-motor for a/c or the heating.
How about housing on the acres (even roofs) of office and industrial park complexes? Would sure cut commuting. On some floors of high-rise office buildings?

How about an economy converted to repairing and restoring anything from appliances to cars rather than waste so much in remanufacture -- the old, merely *component-faulty* thing, being junked in toto.

How about government funded (joint venture paradigm) massive alternative energy projects (especially for fuel)? Solar, bio, Hydrogen, algal, even . . . fuel from feces ?? ("give a shit" !!! Fuel America with the ultimate recycled source)

How about putting people to work cleaning up litter and performing other "municipal" services *for pay sufficient for their health and shelter needs* plus a bit more for minor luxuries -- and even pittance tax-returns into the system? (There can be a viable economy without everything being based on production and consumption of resources – and profit/interest factors)

How about government-business collaboration, also, in "collecting and storing" heat from the square miles of black surfaces of paving or roofing, at least in the cities?

How about hydroponic irrigation in scientific *facilities* (rather than agricultural *fields* before we totally deplete our aquifers?

Does the vast volume of fresh water used in fracking equal an exponential of waste/exploitation of resource (the gas or oil that will be fracked for exploitation) – to feed our exploitation-frenzy for the short term profits?

In the following pages I'll be dealing with these ideas in more detail.

The War Effort (conversion of industries and creation of jobs) for World War II got us out of the Depression. The government funded that.

Now, we need a "Peace Effort" of the same paradigm -- funded by the government to force a transformation from waste and surplus and excess and inflation that has become a complex weapon of economic mass destruction. Our own.

Also, how about realizing that nature may come to be our (**all** of us on the earth) biggest threat. We should develop a global-extent industry manufacturing and stocking for the needs of millions who may need shelter and other aid after natural disasters. We don't need to keep spending on weapons of destruction. We need "weapons of survival"!! How many thousands (at least) of people just in this country could be employed to manufacture modular emergency-housing units – better, panels that would be stored in stacks, then assembled according to size and need of structure, from a one-room on dirt floor shelter – to a field hospital complex.

The excessive discarded clothing now baled and sold as rag-stock-scrap should be the "resource" for an industry and its employees to clean, sort, repair, catalog, package, store, and have ready for shipment anywhere in the world. Much clothing could be reprocessed into blankets fabricated (quilt-like – or "cloth-particleboard-like") **:** sewn- or glued-together pieces of shirts, drapes, pants, whatever . . .

Having reached the level of "magic" in our smart phones and Ipods and such "recreational and gimmicky" things, we should pay millions to manufacture and assemble what *we'd* ***need*** *to survive* in various emergencies.

Perhaps **every** family should have a solar panel at least capable of running LED lighting. Maybe a solar stove too? Just in case. Why it isn't required by law and insurance companies at least in the US and other 1st-World nations . . . that in every home on each floor there's a fire extinguisher . . . . . as well as in every motor vehicle!!!

We, ALL of we, are not ill-prepared for disaster. We're non-prepared. Homeland security?? A farce of futility. The recent NY disaster should be revelation .

Think of all the jobs that can be created in creating the means for us to keep our jobs – and homes – and even lives. And to help others with theirs.

YEAH!! (some introductory comments)

Yeah, things are bad. I've recently read the number of people known to be without jobs is 20-something million. That figure includes those who, for the moment at least, have given up looking. I don't know whether the figures are "guesstimates" or "valid statistical extrapolations" added to the sum of the "known" jobless, perhaps 17 million, cited in surveys.

Another figure I just recently read was 15 million out of work. This is a different known "known" total. Fifteen million people are actively seeking employment is better than 17 . . . but still a huge number unemployed.

Not good. And although the percentage of the unemployed has dropped from over 8 to a little less, that's still an awful lot of people without jobs.

Something's got to be done about providing jobs.

Jobs pay wages.

Without wages, people receive government assistance -- or they'd join the already homeless -- even starve. Bad enough how many have lost their homes. Worse would it be without the government providing *survival* for **its** populace. Without such "socialistic" (read, "humanitarian") emergency-intervention there would be such hardship and worse, that there would be unrest and worse. And let things come to WORST and there might no longer be the government!! Precedents? French Revolution. Russian, Cuba . . . And many more recent elsewheres around the world

There recently were two Presidential candidates. The economy, specifically jobs, was the primary concern of both. Get people back to work, for that will get money earned to be spent as the fuel for commerce -- thus the engine of the economy will at least run smoothly. Maybe just as well if it doesn't again rev! It seems, ever since Reagan, the rev-olution of affluent consumerism for all was primarily running on a fuel of fumes -- credit/debt-spending. And the ascent into the atmosphere of real estate prices ("equity-affluence" assumed from inflation) was fueled by fallacious institutional investments -- and outright fraudulent private sector mortgage originators such as Countrywide (and there were myriad others even colluding with ratings agencies to which they paid bribes for Triple A ratings).

Alas, for the while now, the economy has been significantly misfiring, though not actually stalled (as happened in the Depression when droves stood in lines for food and verily populations of men took to the roads and the rails, perhaps to find work, at least to not be another mouth to feed by staying with their families. Myriad banks and businesses closed, compared to the few in this Great Recession. We need a system, not more of a cesstem that seemed flush, but got flushed.

Two candidates there were. Two "platforms". Obama's focused on the actual, though slow and insufficient, revival of economy during his administration. Down from over 8% unemployed. Provision of government largesse-life-support to major banking institutions. Also loans for 2/3 of the auto industry, GM and Chrysler -- saved at least thousands of jobs. (Ford was in "terminal" state too, but obtained private bailout funding, part of the collateral being the Ford logo copyright.)The Obama administration's platform and presentation was what it had done during the last going-on four years. Things better than they were, but not better enough. He projected that, given another term, he can keep things moving toward recovery. The one specific "big-ticket" he proposed (not promised in one debate) was to hire 100,000 teachers.

Any specific areas of mass-reemployment of the masses otherwise was not really mentioned in the Presidential or VP debates.

Romney made promises, promises. Going to get America back to work. Going to provide jobs. Stimulate the economy. Keep those tax "incentives" that Bush put in place -- in place -- so to perpetuate the amazing jump-start of the economy that they initiated . . . ??? Quite a few years since Bush's tax breaks as "Corporation catalysts" and, the while, we went into this Great Recession. Maybe I should call the tax breaks "fuses for the fireworks of hire-works" (jobs supposed to be created by tax-relief incentive for business expansion). The fuse (tax breaks) was lit, oh yes. But it seems either it wasn't connected, or the fireworks supposed to detonate were a dud -- or all in foreign countries!

But now, no matter, Romney was going to be the savior of the "Middle Class" of working America. Jobs. America back to work.

WHAT JOBS???

Now it's Barack's question. **WHAT JOBS ???**

Perhaps Mitt felt he didn't need to specify. He pointed out that he'd been a successful businessman, running companies (including running them out of existence -- and offshore), thus has the experience and qualifications and credentials to properly handle the *business* of the government. (But at the same time his stance was that the government has no business being the bailout or even benefactor of business!!) -- *except, it seems, via subsidies to the mega-sector such as Agriculture, Petroleum, and outright blatant paying for the whole Military-Industrial Complex.*

Again, other than those paid for by the government, WHAT JOBS??

Anyone . . . . **W H A T J O B S ?????**

The number of government-funded programs Mitt intended to cut would have put a sizeable number of people out of work -- thus adding to the ones who already need jobs! But for Obama to keep funding all those domestic programs will mean increasing the already trillion$-drastic deficit.

Romney proposed to drill for oil. Offshore. Onshore including wilderness and wildlife preserves. Federal land, Private land. More oil drilling. More domestic production (thus depletion of) **our** energy reserves.

But to what extent any increase of Jobs!!! Obama had to consider this too, for he seems to advocate increasing (to some extent) utilization of our own energy resources, thus decreasing our "foreign dependence".

But how many of the unemployed millions can be hired for (or be able to work on) oil rigs or platforms? I'm only guessing here, but let's say an oil platform involves 500 jobs: those actually on and running the thing, others servicing it, providing supplies of various kinds from hardware to food, and transportation of equipment and for workers' needs, etc. So per platform or land-based facility we'd have 500 people put back to work.

To get 500,000 people in oil drilling jobs we'll need 1,000 oil drilling facilities!!

Well, if we go with the 15 million unemployed figure that leaves 14 million five hundred thousand people still looking for jobs that Mitt, in the debate, was so enthusiastically and animatedly promising to provide.

Now it's Barack's responsibility.

"Clean coal"! Mitt specified that, too, in a debate. How long will that last now that we're, so to speak, performing mountain mastectomies to get it, rather than "linear lumpectomies", the former procedures of actually mining?

And, coal, oil, or other, wouldn't it be wiser to keep what we got just in case our great grand children might need it? All these "conventional" energy resources -- we know they're there and we have proven technologies to extract them, transport, convert them to fuel. Some of which will always be needed such as for major industrial processes, motors, etc. even if alternative energy systems become viable.

But what if alternatives don't work out . . . . ? The preserved conventional resources would have to become "alternatively productive" by the hyper-efficiency of future engines, generators, heating, etc. (Or society would have to revert to a former way of life!!)

Mitt considered natural resources to be commodities, mere products, their immediate primary value in putting people to work to make money -- but also to make profits for business!!

Barack?? We're listening. Good luck pumping more petro and gas prices going back down to where they *once* were. What need? People are in rampantly wasteful mobility (and rush-hour immobility) even with the present prices.

And wouldn't it be far better to continue increasing fuel efficiency, thus decreasing fuel consumption (requiring more drilling)? If you're getting 30% more mpg, prices can go up 30% and you're even!! If you're driving back and forth to work in a "commuta-car" (one of my listed suggestions at the beginning of this writing) and you're getting the equivalent of 200 mpg, $6 per gallon gas would still leave you saving money from what you're spending now to drive that $25,000+ combination space-capsule and yacht through the traffic, maybe achieving (given the stop-and-start) well less than 10 mpg?

Jobs. Mitt-jobs. Obama jobs. Job-jobs.

WHAT JOBS ??

Mitt didn't specify or list or enumerate or suggest.

Except . . . .

He'd get that pipeline built!!!

That's the pipeline from Canada which, it seems is being blocked because it's routed over a major American aquifer. There's proven possibility of catastrophic spillage (BP, Caribbean -- prior, Exxon Valdez -- and in between, many little pipe leaks). In view of even the slight percentile (distance of pipeline over aquifer/overall length of pipeline), to chance petro-pollution of precious (and diminishing) fresh water . . . is not just unconscionable but, from a broad business perspective, reckless. (From an environmental standpoint, criminal!!)

But that pipeline he was going to get built because it would provide jobs. Of the fourteen million three hundred thousand people **not** back to work (500,000 drilling oil + I'm proposing an arbitrary 200,000 involved with that "clean coal" = 14,300,000 still unemployed) . . . how many of them would become pipe-fitters and fill the associated and ancillary and support positions to bring in the *Canadian oil*?

If it's so important to build the pipeline, just what's the problem with re-routing it? A little lengthier? Maybe that'll require a few more jobs!!

More people back to work. A thought for you now, Barack?

More imported energy. From Canada. Already our major "foreign" source. (What happened to that "American energy independence" bit? (Maybe Mitt's heavily invested in Canadian shale?)

OPEC provides a smaller percentage to the multi-national petro-"pool" deriving from a globalized distribution of major oil cartel-controlled drilling sites. There's already a whole lot of drilling going on. Now add more domestic production too, what with all the U. S. drilling on- and off-shore that anyone proposes? There would be a lot more of petro-products (gas and diesel etc.) on the market. Maybe prices would come down some?

If so, consumption would increase, no doubt, as people would just drive more and more. And there'd be less concern about shutting off lights what with lower electric bills. "Conservation? For what?? It's cheap again!!! USE IT UP!!!! We've put so many people back to work drilling and trucking and in the tourism business is booming again, etc. Everyone's making money to go out and buy more stuff too, so much of it made in part from petroleum. Let's use it up!! It makes money!!"

It's ours!! Our energy "independence" is the short-sighted, profit-driven, private sector perspective!! American oil production must be increased. GET IT OUT!! USE IT UP!! Same with coal. Natural gas. The latter seems to be potentially the biggest energy reserve. Vast pockets of natural gas to be tapped -- one projection being 200 years'-worth at present usage. **That's enough for a little over 2 generations hence!!**

Domestic petroleum reserves? Seems there's not as much as gas.

Coal? Probably even less.

"Conventional energy sources" are FINITE resources. Depleted, they're depleted. Gone, they're gone. Their chemical/molecular formulation took millions of years.

But the one party's platform proposed to pump and mine and frack and lower price to increase consumption . . . . . talk about self-centered, short-term, stupidity!!

Political idiocy because it panders to pathology, not mere profiteering, in "patriotism's" concept-euphemism.

Crude Oil and Total Petroleum Imports Top 15 Countries

Crude Oil and Total Petroleum Imports Top 15 Countries

September 2011 Import Highlights: Released November 29, 2011 Monthly data on the origins of crude oil imports in September 2011 has been released and it shows that three countries exported more than 1,000 thousand barrels per day to the United States (see table below). The top five exporting countries accounted for 69 percent of United States crude oil imports in September while the top ten sources accounted for approximately 88 percent of all U.S. crude oil imports. The top five sources of US crude oil imports for September were Canada (2,324 thousand barrels per day), Saudi Arabia (1,465 thousand barrels per day), Mexico (1,099 thousand barrels per day), Venezuela (759 thousand barrels per day) and Nigeria (529 thousand barrels per day). The rest of the top ten sources, in order, were Colombia (510 thousand barrels per day), Iraq (403 thousand barrels per day), Ecuador (299 thousand barrels per day), Angola (283 thousand barrels per day) and Russia (275 thousand barrels per day). Total crude oil imports averaged 9,006 thousand barrels per day in September, which is a decrease of (16) thousand barrels per day from August 2011.

Canada remained the largest exporter of total petroleum in September, exporting 2,829 thousand barrels per day to the United States, which is an increase from last month (2,637 thousand barrels per day). The second largest exporter of total petroleum was Saudi Arabia with 1,479 thousand barrels per day.

Crude Oil Imports (Top 15 Countries)
(Thousand Barrels per Day)

Country	Sep-11	Aug-11	YTD 2011	Sep-10	YTD 2010
CANADA	2,324	2,240	2,157	1,937	1,971
SAUDI ARABIA	1,465	1,075	1,180	1,082	1,072
MEXICO	1,099	1,150	1,113	1,108	1,132
VENEZUELA	759	806	893	919	928
NIGERIA	529	854	826	1,107	1,018
COLOMBIA	510	365	364	308	328
IRAQ	403	637	473	422	464
ECUADOR	299	303	203	229	215
ANGOLA	283	311	323	404	413
RUSSIA	275	252	246	286	295
BRAZIL	163	213	225	177	270
KUWAIT	145	165	164	172	204
ALGERIA	139	140	204	366	337
CHAD	74	32	54	30	14
OMAN	72	52	39	0	0

Total Imports of Petroleum (Top 15 Countries)
(Thousand Barrels per Day)

Country	Sep-11	Aug-11	YTD 2011	Sep-10	YTD 2010
CANADA	2,829	2,637	2,670	2,479	2,537
SAUDI ARABIA	1,479	1,075	1,187	1,093	1,086
MEXICO	1,192	1,185	1,218	1,254	1,260
VENEZUELA	806	906	979	1,008	1,007
RUSSIA	592	585	609	648	624
NIGERIA	580	892	876	1,174	1,053
COLOMBIA	529	395	395	363	360
IRAQ	404	637	473	422	464
ECUADOR	305	309	205	229	217
ANGOLA	304	331	335	417	422
ALGERIA	291	298	396	543	512
VIRGIN ISLANDS	189	185	189	302	261
BRAZIL	188	228	240	181	289
ARUBA	149	81	79	0	0
KUWAIT	145	165	165	172	206

Note: The data in the tables above exclude oil imports into the U.S. territories.

Eh, why should Romney, as representation of ethics and ethos of his echelon (and party), give a damned about so distant a future as that of his childrens' childrens' children or even sooner? There's so much money to be made **now** if people are back to production, making money to go into the corporate coffers via their consumption for production for consumption.

But there's another argument that's been given for "drill America" (bringing to mind a "shaft" -- also regarding exploiting conventional coal mining). This second delusion (the first that the unemployment crisis would be solved) is that by becoming "energy-independent", America will be more secure.

First, terminating our consumption of foreign energies would mean our independence, yes . . . for the *while we so greatly increased the exploitation and depletion of our own domestic reserves*.

But, **second**, revenue to foreign sources of petroleum at least provides for their regimes, even if little benefits their people. But it would be the "regimes" that would recruit from the rank and file the insurgents and terrorists, or establish actual militias or military -- and become "operant enemy states" vs. America -- if we shut them off -- and thus they'd have nothing to lose.

Third, from here and there, even including Venezuela (and its dear leader Chavez), we have been *getting* petro. We can even include OPEC in this present paragraph's context of international status, potential threat(?), of "foreign oil" suppliers. What actual, functional, threat do these countries present to the U. S. other than possibly increasing their prices or nationalizing some drill-rig or refinery or something? And if they got too pushy, there's always the Iranian paradigm to pursue -- have the CIA overthrow their government. Somewhat a similar scenario, since, was in Indonesia (Aceh). These "foreign oil" sources are really at the mercy of the all but omnipotent petroleum corporations, ExxonMobil the epitome. Shit happen? Exxon exits. What's it care about one mere trickle-in of global petroleum (or gas) sources?

Fourth, China and even Russia are greater threats to US *supremacy* (economic), hardly at all to national *sovereignty* (unless something brings about military confrontation). Our natural resource (and other) trade (globalism) with them is a form of détente. Not being enemies is beneficial for both sides -- if it's profitable. Terminate that mutually assured economic mutualism (or at least symbiosis) and anyone sane thinks we'd be safer ??

A **fifth** perspective on the global petro sources: say we shut off buying petro from Bmwarbambia in Africa or SanPetdrotonia in So. America in order to be "energy independent"? They'd just sell to the eager buyers of China and Russia (and others). *That would be enhancing our security -- in any way at all??*

So far I've discussed what **does not** solve our present problems.

So far I've indicated that more conventional energy extraction and consumption would result in far more serious future problems.

HOW INDEPENDENT OF FOREIGN ENERGY SOURCES WILL AMERICA BE WHEN IT USES UP ITS OWN RESERVES??

So far I think I've made it obvious that pumping and piping oil and exploiting coal will still leave millions without jobs.

My concern in this writing is that neither of the candidates (nor anyone else) ***seemed to get it.***

The **"it"** is that the very economic system is faulty, fallacious, failed. It's premise is a monetary-perpetual-motion-machine. Its outcome is a Ponzi paradigm, exacerbated by expectation of ever-increasing GDP -- but extraction from monetary circulation into profits, dividends, and immense remunerations which are retained as "wealth", for the wealthy. From whence it doesn't "trickle-down" sufficiently. Obviously of late. Not even a trickle into jobs despite Bush's bucks-breaks-for-boost.

Nobody seems to get . . . IT . .

The crux of the "it" is WHAT KIND OF JOBS otherwise? I'd first asked Mitt. Mining and pumping and piping won't put the nation back to work.

Now Barack, in this second term you'd better get with IT. What kind of jobs can be provided to get this nation back to work, an economic circulation going again, and also a means to siphon down the soaring deficit?

Aspects of the "it" that they *(nobody)* seem to get.

The first (1) of the "subset considerations" of the multiphase "it".

Communism didn't work. Doesn't work. Won't work. From the micro-membership experiments in 19th and early 20th century "utopian" sects and societies in the U. S. we've seen the fallacy and failure. From the catastrophic failures (and atrocities) involved in Russia and China and Cambodia and Cuba and elsewhere we have ample evidence too.

Socialism (2) alone doesn't work. Much the same reason that Communism doesn't. Human <u>nature</u> is an infrastructural absolute, so to speak. Man's basic nature is competitive (his cooperative-unto-altruistic endeavors and acts usually depending on his having attained security (if not supremacy) first. Financial supersedence evolves to philanthropy, for example.

Man's basic nature (3) requires something for his efforts: recognition, respect, remuneration, *reward* in the form of monetary and/or material possession. Take away the arena, the incentive, the goals . . for inspiration, intention, contention, competition, even greed and materialistic or managerial megalomania . . . and things just slump to the least productive as the level of aspiration because that's the *easiest* (kind of like keeping <u>down</u> with the Joneskys on the commune). No system for upward mobility? No incentive for upward mobility!! *Competition*-to-reward for achievement is the dynamic of viable socio-economic system.

(4) Capitalism is Darwinian.

Capitalism is based on ambition, incentive competition.

Capitalism is a dynamic beyond survival of the fittest in that the less than fittest so much survive quite adequately (The Dollar Stores vs. Niemen Marcus, for one off-the-wall extreme example).

Capitalism results in extinction (or obsolescence) of the *very unfit* (or come-to-be outdated due to innovation).

Capitalism is a "binary" system. Management and labor. Seeing them as separate systems, especially adversaries, rather than components of a requisite *single* process (at least symbiosis, ideally synergy) is fallacious, myopic. Without the labor force, what possible value, let alone "worth", would the managerial levels represent? But without management, labor would be a peasantry unless from its ranks a managerial and organizational echelon emerged.

It takes both "sides". There have been swings of exploitation. Way back almost cruel exploitation of workers by robber-barons and their manager-minions. Conditions in mines and mills, garment districts and slaughter-houses have been documented to our horror. Yet there have come to be reciprocal effects of labor demands and management concessions actually resulting in driving enterprises out of business (such as a lot of companies that could no longer afford union wages and benefits -- and obviously, of late, almost the whole automotive industry). American wage-levels and union-won "legacy benefits" (ongoing after retirement) resulted in the "exploitation of management". This, in part, resulted in driving enterprises out of the country to foreign places where dirt-cheap wages represented survival income to people no longer able to all survive as peasants. (Of course greater corporate profits, not just the corporation's survival, significantly factored in the off shoring too).

Capitalism's give and take (or labor-management reciprocities of take and take) are part of a viable, "natural" system.

But, *laissez faire*, uncontrolled (for such market forces do become uncontrollable -- like warfare) . . . "dog-eat-dog" dynamics not only defeat the least fit. Through the deluded daring of the Alpha level ascension of the "market" (such as investment banks). . . . the whole system came close to collapse -- had it not been for Federal money to keep the private sector from domino-implosion. Through greed and fraud and extortion major capitalistic endeavors have been destroyed by the private enterprises (the people) controlling them (prime examples were mining companies, railroads, etc.)

We may have very high unemployment, but we're surely not in a 2nd Depression

But we have a huge number of people out of work.

And we've heard what almost seems platform hypocrisy -- Mitt so much condemned Obama's "trickle-down government", but Mitt's promise to put America back to work . . . which he, even in his multi-millionaire, industrialist-investor private-sector expertise, had contributed nothing toward . . . . . but would accomplish only if he became the head of the government!!!

Government leases lands and waters for drilling. Cheap. Government pays the military budget, thus provides federal funding of military industrial complex in all its complexity and billions.

But, as I think is obvious (without my having pointed it out above), any increasing employment in these areas will only be a trickle-out from the unemployment lines.

So again I ask, WHAT OTHER JOBS?

There was the Depression.

Banks failed, one after the other.

Businesses closed.

The economy went into "collateral arrest" or something like that.

Now let's consider this dire scenario and say that any remedy or renaissance of the country rested solely on what the private sector would do. Even if the fortunes of the fortunate were provided as "seed money" to re-start manufacturing and commerce, and also provide mortgage relief to keep farmers on land and people in homes . . . . even with the contribution of all their millions, the millionaires could not have provided enough to prime the pump of the whole populace's prosperity!! Not even their mere survival.

IT TOOK THE GOVERNMENT.

It wasn't a socialistic insurgency or conspiracy.

It was economic salvation from the curse of uncontrolled Capitalism's free-market overheated mania-become a melt-down massacre of the economy!!.

No, he was not a Saint Roosevelt. He was surely but a secular Savior Roosevelt. His radio chats were but great public relations, personalizing the Presidency for the people. His programs putting people back to work building walls and taking photographs and repairing roads and all (WPA the best known of them) were completely insufficient to put the whole nation back to work and to restore an economic system. (We have here a precedent for perceiving the present percentage of re-employment only through oil drilling or infrastructure repair "recovery programs").

Back then, how many cemetery walls could be built? Roads repaired? Pictures taken? Paintings painted? Etc? Farming revision and reorientation (such as contour plowing) for the "dust bowl survivors" provided precious but paltry economic stimulus. Even with the larger projects such as Blue Ridge Highway, proportionately few were put back to work. Other large public works projects such as the Hoover Dam helped but a small segment of a destitute national populace.

To get things moving out of the Great Depression IT TOOK THE GOVERNMENT'S most massive ENTERPRISE . . . . .

THE WAR EFFORT!!

No, the government itself didn't set up shop to make tanks and guns and ammunition and aircraft and all in converted halls of congress or even the Pentagon.The government massively funded private enterprises to convert from peacetime manufacture to wartime production. And with government funding, these enterprises re-employed the thousands and thousands who were not taken into the military itself. The female-workforce, the "Rosie the riveters" (and all the other military manufacture capacities of employment) were earning their wages **from the government** (which paid for the war-effort conversions and costs of the private sector companies). Those companies wrote the pay checks, yes. But they were paying-out what the federal government had paid-in!

That was then. There was a war going on already. There isn't now. In the paradigm of "conventional warfare" we could get involved back then. Perhaps we should have before. But the "theaters" of the war were far from our shores, which were separated from Europe and Japan by oceans.

Now, what's a mere ocean? ICBMs are probably not as much of a worry as would be individuals with suicidal motivations as synergy to whatever weaponry or viral-ry they might be carrying on an inbound commercial flight.

No, the present world is no place to start a war to provide jobs.

Any massive military buildup would not only be counter-productive from the standpoint of "threatening" -- thus switching that "détente-mutualism" of trade competition (such as with China – an alms race) to an "arms-race".

And in the present paradigm of threats by any nation, spending billions on massive conventional weaponry would be spending billions on obsolescence!! Yes, we have to maintain advanced and sufficient conventional armed forces (land, sea, air, and on foot). But "maintain" may be the pertinent term here. Billions for *higher*-tech etc. may be no more effective in our "strength" vs. aggressor threat -- than billions for exploring moon or mars would be for our "survival" in case of approaching meteor.

The economy is not going to be resuscitated by the government's conversion to militaristic manufacturing of the auto industries or appliance manufacturers or any other major employers from whom people have been laid off.

So far I've noted that drilling and mining and even neo-militarism won't put the country back to work.

SO WHAT JOBS WILL ??

The jobs created by the new effort to defeat the present enemy -- unemployment!!

WE MUST MOBILIZE

A PEACE EFFORT

The *government* must provide the economic "surge" to start us on the road to an economic victory -- an economic and employment revitalization through productivity and product innovations.

And not just the "conventional 'alternatives' (wind, solar, etc.)" .

But why not just put people back to work doing what they were doing before, if government is going to provide the "mobilization" funding?

For one reason (1), because we shouldn't use resources for what we don't really need more of -- and are running out of room to dispose of. This surplus and excess of stuff so much comprises "retail". And (2) most of that manufacture actually takes place in other countries, much to the advantage of major US corporations such as Walmart, electronics, toys, trinkets, and you-name-it, because of cheap wages -- and the "false-advantage" to the American consumers of cheap prices. Savings at the cash register has, in part, cost our domestic economy its jobs so that people don't have anything to spend because they don't have incomes from jobs any more!

But mainstream economic "logic" would advocate bringing back more and more of those jobs making more and more of that plastic stuff (and all the rest that everyone's got to get, then tries to get rid of at the yard sale. Consumer goods for consumer consumption, the more the bigger the job base for the workers and bottom line for investors.

But, again, almost all those jobs are off-shored.

How, pray tell, would the off-shored jobs be brought back to our shores? Tariffs to force those corporations to bring home their employees? No chance, for that would force American retail to raise prices in order to pay American workers. For if they were able to maintain labor costs equivalent to abroad, the American workers (1) wouldn't work for such pittance, and (2) if they did, wouldn't earn enough to have sufficient disposable income to be proportionate consumers for the products they'd be producing here!!!!

Global labor is here to stay. Rather, global labor is "**<u>there</u>** to stay".

But what about here?

The mobilization of the new "war-effort" here? The "Peace-effort".

What would be the areas of employment in the realm of "unconventional 'alternatives' "?

At this point I'll stop analysis and dissertation.

At this point it's ideas not just to put people back in jobs and earning money. The ideas I'm going to present would save money and save resources, all the while providing nationwide (and beyond) opportunities for the private sector whose enterprises would be the actual employers, manufacturers, installers.

Like the WW II mobilization effort, the present Peace Mobilization Effort though the manufacturing transitions, retooling, revisions and such would be private-sector. . . the capital "surge" to get these new systems of systems (and such) instated . . . *would come from the Federal Government.*

Call it socialistic. Go ahead. Socialistic it would be in somewhat the same way as government subsidies to agriculture and technology and pharmaceuticals and airlines and railroads and rapid transit systems and schools and public service employment and interstate highways and much more. There would be three differences: Many of the categories I just mentioned require *continuing* subsidies in order to stay in business.

My ideas (1) would not be ongoing life-support systems (such as farm subsidies or "federalization" of railroads and airlines etc. They'd be enhancements of our ways of life and systems of living that would become self-sustaining. And (2) the R&D and manufacture and installation and implementation of these "neo-mobilization" (I'll call them) efforts would provide capitalistic returns, profits, to the private enterprises involved. Thus economic-system flow: wages, spending, tax bases, profits, dividends, a flow between the multi-level reservoir and lesser "containments" of the economy. Finally (3) these ideas and products and systems would save a fortune in conventional energy costs/causes and pollution/results.

But there needs to be the incentive of government funding to enterprises to hire and manufacture and install such new devices and systems on a "mobilization" scale. And also to assist consumers in being able to purchase such things . . . . . and, lastly, price controls to keep the "surge" from becoming an inflation.

Best I get to the ideas. The innovations. The systems-inventions.
Quite a few are already in existence.

Such as things that let in *direct sunlight* as the source of solar powered lighting!!

One such device is called a "skylight". They come in all sizes and shapes and various materials. They're already manufactured and distributed, but used rather sparingly. One here and there on houses. And on those vast expanses of flat warehouse or big-box store roofs there may be a few. Seen from below, within the commercial buildings, except on exceptionally cloudy days, enough light comes from the rare skylight that it pretty well matches the illumination from an electricity-powered fluorescent fixture. Were there as many skylights as there usually are light fixtures, there'd hardly be need for electricity for lighting during the day.

To retrofit roofs with skylights would put a whole lot of people to work in established skylight-making industry, and contractors on roofs cutting rectilinear holes and installing them. And think of the electricity that would be saved.

To roof anything, is it really necessary to block out the sun and sky? Surely with the miracles of plastics and carbon fiber and other interfaced technology, transparent roofing could be developed. Sunny day, open louvers and let the (yes, ***fusion**-reaction solar powered*) light flood into the warehouse or store or even office, school, whatever.

So many people would go to work in the new industry of see-through roofing. And there'd be a lot making the louver devices to control just how much light (and with it heat) would come on down.

In other situations, a product (one called Solatube) is like an 8" or bigger duct, but highly reflective inside so that the light entering from above is "bounced" even through bends and fittings to emerge, almost bulb-bright, inside the structure. (Think fiber-optic cable made very large).

This system of "ducting light" should be mass marketed and even mandated, to let the sun take the place (at least partially) of the coal-fired (or even Nat'l gas) generating plants. And so many jobs would be created making the tubes, transporting, installing. With more R&D it might be possible to duct sunlight even into lower floors of high-rises. One way would be with enhanced reflectivity ducts all the way from top down. An alternative would be to have "collectors" (think a kind of satellite-dish setup) on sun-side of building, supplying even just the floor its collector is on the outside wall of.

But of course we should continue producing solar panels to convert sunlight into electricity, not just surrogate electric lighting. I see more and more panels in my travels.

With separate circuitry just for lighting or techno re-charging, etc., and for the illumination of L. E. Ds, it seems one could have a small bank of panels on the roof to provide total power, either directly to fixtures, or via a battery bank to store charge for times of dark or insufefficient sunlight. (Aside from acres-spreads of solar panels only here or there, I see single panels atop or beside innumerable highway signals and signs, temporary for construction sites, and permanent as well.

Had the government provided farm- or military-industrial -type subsidy to Solectra or Solyndra or those other such "fool's investments in boondoggles" . . . a lot of people would be at work making and installing the solar systems that surely seem to be at least viable "collaborating alternatives" with (though not total replacements of) generator plant electricity. And eventually such jump-started companies probably would have become self-sufficient, even profitable.

Solar and wind generation of DC current (thereby allowing storage), would also entail constructing and wiring "centralized grids" to provide electricity for the "light-demand-uses" of illumination and tech. A bank of panels or roof-top turbine (preferably both as a "binary" system), might make each building, even house, a self-powered unit (except for the electric stove, heat, or air conditioning, which would still circuit from the conventional grid).

The setup would be somewhat like where someone has a stand-by generator in case of power-outage. Only rather than a single circuitry for everything in the house (or other building), the conventional grid would feed a high demand circuit: stove, heat, a.c.. The rest of the wiring could stay as is for heavy electrical demands. But the lighting and light-demand "alternative" power source (s) would require a separate wiring setup. Think how many electrical jobs would be created.

Single building or "cluster-grid" (neighborhood or city "block") alternative systems could be powered by solar panels and wind, both to charge a battery bank (from which lights and light-demand usage otherwise would get power). Obviously it would be DC. Within short distances it would be functional, and storable!!

There would be no need for huge, exorbitantly expensive, wind turbines. On the roofs could be far smaller propeller-types -- or even other systems such as "squirrel-cage" blade configurations to catch the wind. With reduced cost of equipment, even several turbines on one building could be installed. Where there's wind, there's wind from one side of a structure to the other . . . completely.

And, of course, conversion to LEDs should be required as much as possible. Think how bright the LED from a little flashlight run off three triple-A batteries!!

Also, we should use far fewer lights!! That we saturate areas with illumination is absolutely unnecessary for satisfactory perception and adequate vision. We actually "wash-out" the potential of far more creative and restful, perhaps even mental-healthy, contrasts of bright and dim, "photo-aesthetic" atmospheres in our homes, offices, even factories and shopping buildings.

In a world of increasing population but decreasing water resources (due, in part to global-warming/de-glaciation thus decrease in river-flow volume) . . . that purer water than what most of that world's population has to drink is used by the advanced nations for sewage . . . . . is unconscionable. Criminal!!!

All urinals should be waterless by law. Already they're being installed in various places such as highway rest areas. They should be everywhere. Look at all the jobs making them and replacing the flush-ones. There might come to be a lot of jobs reprocessing the ceramic material of the removed ones into some kind of aggregate.

Toilets per se should use only "grey water" -- that which has been collected from the rain on the roof and, as well, from the sinks (and in residential realms, even from the washing machine and dishwasher).

This would entail dual-system plumbing. Wastewater would be stored in a tank which would feed to the toilets. Pure water would come from the faucets, yes, but then would drain into the "gray-water" cistern from which it would be pumped to the toilet water tanks.

Think of the jobs that such innovation of preservation of our most precious resource (water) would create!! Think the precedent -- back in the late 1800s when plumbing itself was introduced and had to be installed from scratch in buildings of all kinds.

The same massive conversion, of course, installed gas-lighting pipe-systems in buildings, then replaced them with wiring for electrical lighting. All from scratch!! So obviously it could be done with innovative new systems such as I'm considering here.

The possibility of converting water toilets to composting units should be researched, prototyped, experimented.

Still seem too big an undertaking? Consider the nation-wide installation of the fibers and wires and all so that you can watch your cable TV networks!!!

Sewage. If we're still going to have it (rather than individual-unit composting) rather than just gather it and treat it, why not convert this universally available resource into energy? With the right "digestion" process, shit yields methane. Though a worse greenhouse gas than CO_2 methane can be used to power combustion engines (or be burned to produce steam for turbines).

Doubtful that there'll ever come a complete conversion of toilet-tech so that one's bolus goes into a container to be collected for the energy digester -- rather than goes kersplush into a bowl of water to be flushed. But from the confluence of the sewer pipes and regional pumps, the resource, now just "treated" at existing facilities, could be converted. Various whole systems of "sewage treatment" are already installed and in operation in almost all the world's urban areas. All that would be required for shit-to-energy production would be the final processing.

Think of the jobs manufacturing sewage digester systems!!

Think of the slogan to make people aware of their contribution to a new fuel-energy resource . . . "Give a shit!!"

There's no chance people are going to give up their conventional automobiles with all those bells and whistles and automatic features including almost self-parking now, I believe. The ultimate absurdity of hyper-technological indulgence is the self-driving car. It's under development!!

But to go back and forth through stop and start (or at least creeping) rush hour traffic in such costly luxury? Does it make sense, considering the thing has an engine that can make it go 65 mph legally -- much faster actually, and thus a factor of its fuel *inefficiency* in traffic jams is costing the driver, and the environment?

How about fully enclosed golf-cart type "commuta-car", its electric motor run off the kind of batteries that are used in fork lifts or pallet jacks (thus readily on the market). A few safety features, perhaps a propane heating device, a radio, . . . who needs much more to go the 30 or so miles to and then back from where the thing is parked all day (at work) and all night (back at home).

Think of all the jobs making the "commuta-cars". Think of the extent to which the components are already on the market -- as golf carts, material-handling-equipment motors, batteries, etc.

Priced right, think how many people would spend in order to quickly save more than the thing would cost as the alternative to the conventional car for commuting. And used so much less, the car itself would last that much longer!! Thus the prices of fully-equipped cars could be raised, loan-durations lengthened, to maintain economies of profit for the auto industry.

The level of complexity/luxury of a car is almost beyond logic. The life-span of a car is too short. One major component (or some extent of body deterioration) and the whole, perhaps 95% actually intact, functional device is remanded to the junk yard. Such waste (and of appliances too) is horrendous. Criminal!!!

But for those who would still use the car-car to and from and within the city (this would include cabs and delivery vehicles, etc.) there should be the after-market shut-down systems mandated. Come to a stop over X number of seconds and the engine shuts off. Touch the gas pedal to resume motion and instantly it resumes internal combustion operation.

That hundreds of vehicles stopped in traffic have their 4, 5, 6, or 8 cylinders all firing away turning gasoline or diesel into carbon atmospherics is criminal, adding to the insult of using up finite fuel resources to go nowhere so much.

The hundreds (probably thousands) of people who could be put to work manufacturing and installing idle-shutoff systems would be a boost to the economy.

Shouldn't the next "generation" of "conventional cars" (not the bare-bones commuta-car I've mentioned) . . shouldn't they all be hybrid? You have a gasoline or diesel engine (and hopefully, eventually alternative fuels). That engine runs a generator which **charges a battery** *(such as those already running material handling equipment like forklifts all day*). Either directly from the generator or from the battery(s), power goes to electric motors, one driving each of the four wheels. No need for all those gears and shafts and the manufacturing cost and frictional waste involved. Four wheel drive without any need for "differential gearing". Braking contributes to re-charging the battery.

Come to a stop and nothing has to be running (except for radio or heater, etc.) But no need for engine operation when nothing's moving otherwise!! Basing electric drive on engine-generator re-charge of conventional equipment battery should provide a driving range comparable to standard combustion-engine-driven vehicle of today. Engine to charge battery (hybrid system) should allow conventional equipment batteries to be used. So the battery has to recharge from the engine perhaps within 100 miles? The vehicle would just keep moving, occupants hardly noticing the engine has gone on because electric motors make the vehicle move.

For charging by gas or diesel motor, fuel system is already world-wide in place. You'd still stop at the "gas station" even with an electricity-driven vehicle.

Automobiles should be even less expensive, assuming some of the astoundingly excess options were deleted -- such as 40-way adjustable individual-buttock-sensing heated seats, separate climate-zones, partial self-parking provision, variable suspension, 4,000 watt (at least) Bose sound systems etc. etc. etc. Wouldn't it be preferable to reemploy people making whole-concept functional vehicles for future needs -- and, yes, wants (such as depletions) . . . not wants (such as "gotta haves" such superficial, energy-consuming, expensive, almost ridiculous luxury features.)

Where there are frequent traffic lights, there should be sensor systems (or timing) so that when the red you're at turns green, the light you approach turns green, and the next, and the next. Years and years ago in New York City this timing seemed to be the case along the major avenues. Start at one light, maintain speed, and you could make it through numerous ones consecutively turning green for your approach.

So often I now drive at the prescribed speed limit through sections where every one of 4 or 5 lights will turn red just as I get to it. With the technology available that's insane as well as wasteful of fuel and polluting of the air (and likely damage to the drivers' emotional stabilities and cardio-vascular systems).

If so many of those roadside temporary and permanent signs are powered by a single solar panel, it would seem that almost all highway lighting could be. Those that are already wired could be circuited to be powered only by the solar panel as long as there would be sufficient sunlight to keep the battery-pack charged. Otherwise the conventional wiring and electrical source would provide power.

Think of the jobs making the panels and doing the dual wiring systems.

In numerous cases as I drive in the dark, I notice that the illumination from reflective surfaces (signs, markers, reflectors per se,) along the roads and intersections -- is brighter than that from the electric lights. Some of the latter are almost sky-high on the interstates exchanges.

Also, factor in the intensity of headlights now.

And consider that if there's no one on the road in an area, there's really no need for lighting at all!!

So why all that electricity burned all night long? Even if it's from solar power??

Perhaps some innovative expansion of reflectivity as actual illumination (not just delineation) would be functional -- and provide jobs -- and income for the workers and profit for companies involved.

That people embark on their mini-migrations from home to work and back every day results from what we defined as progress. Progress was to live in suburbia, an hour's drive away from work. Two hours daily (at least) taken up away from the time one could be home with family or activities otherwise. Time sitting in the luxury of the consuming and fuming highway-paradigm vehicle (again, some cars surely seem a fusion of space-capsule and yacht). Costing $50, $60, or more a week for the gas. Then the parking in the city. The depreciation.

That adds up to a lot of money spent to creep along and be frustrated by "rush" hour sclerotic clotting (the traffic and one's own cardio-vascular damage?).

More and more should be able to "tele-commute". If one can sit in a cubicle with a computer in an office building, should one not be able to function just as well in a room with a computer in his home?

But, an alternative -- in how many cases could office buildings be converted to contain housing? High-rise-with-a-view housing for those who work on the commercial floors of the building? The utilities systems are already installed but for "branches" to apartments' kitchens or bathrooms. Dwelling floors could be anywhere within the structure, probably the higher up the higher price. The employer could function as landlord too, perhaps providing the "in-house" housing as part of pay arrangement.

On the roof could be combination park/playground, solar collection, maybe garden plot. On the residential floors there could be public areas for exercise or other recreation.

Up in the morning, eat breakfast, dress, and walk to the elevator.

Think of the money and resources saved. Think of the pollution abated.

Think of the jobs creating the "mixed-use" conversions of, now, just office buildings. Also consider that most of those buildings are now unoccupied during the night. All those hours of heating goes to waste, multiplied by all those hours the commuted-home employee heats his suburban house. Residential/commercial high rise buildings surely seem a cost-effective way to put a lot of construction people back to work as well as to save energy resources.

And out in the suburbs there are those vast campuses of "garden-apartment-format" office and industrial parks. So much land. Why not build condo-housing on some of the lawns? Why not on those acres of flat roofs?

The employment domain would become the residential as well. Up in the morning, off on foot across the walkway -- or down from the rooftop housing.

Think of the time saved for living, rather than commuting!!

Think of the money saved. The petro saved. Thus the de facto vast reduction in gasoline costs (because, not commuting, one wouldn't be using much of any!!!)

Think of all the jobs building the campus-condos.

But a further matter concerning traveling the highways.

In so many places, come twice a day, the times of the clog.

Traffic is moving along at 65, so well-spaced it could well be congealed into two of the three lanes without crowding. But all three lanes of scattered cars race along until they come upon where cars from another road merge. Almost suddenly, last minute, due to the merging cars (these bumper-to-bumper), the three highway lanes try to squeeze into two.

And everything comes to a start-stop, creep, cut-in clot for fifteen or twenty minutes. Then, the merges merged, suddenly everything's back in three lanes at full speed limit.

Think how many jobs could be created by instituting a system of lane-shift far ahead of the merge. The three lanes thus "preemptively meshed together into two lanes without slowing, would continue to race along while the merging traffic would have its own "entry-lane" (the right, vacated one) in which to achieve highway speed, themselves, before meshing into the other lanes -- or staying put in the right lane!

Maybe electrical signaling would be the way, starting at least a couple miles from the merge. "All traffic begin merge into left two lanes unless exiting highway at the next interchange". That's what the solar-powered sign would order. "Violators subject to $500 fine". And there would be cameras!! Think of the jobs installing such systems to save so much wasted time, fuel, and atmospheric waste/pollution. An alternative, more expensive, would be to actually create a couple miles' length extra access lane from the merge.

In a couple cases I frequently traverse, there are *two* lanes of merge that clog into the three lanes of highway. At the very least, the merge traffic should be funneled down to one lane before joining the highway. The interstate highway system is mostly a marvel -- except for its interchanges which are horrifically outdated, obsolete, insufficient, inefficient. Inane!!

Traditional cloverleaf configurations were designed for much lighter traffic. "Gridlock of swirls" seems to be the situation at the height of rush hour. Traffic exiting one highway has to merge with that of the highway being entered, that lane of which is trying to exit. And this becomes a four-way fallacy of design. At least at the major intersections (4 or 5 in the Boston, Mass. area), clover leaf interchanges should be replaced with egress and entry ramps so that traffic merges onto entered highway beyond the interchange. Yes, such reconfiguration and reconstruction would cost many millions. But think of the jobs. And think of the taxable incomes those jobs would provide. Think of the after-tax disposable income to be spent into the varied aspects of consumer-economy!!!

And . . . . put in the context of the original purpose of the interstate highway system -- national defense -- wouldn't such upgrade of such a strategic threat as gridlock traffic (ohmy god, what if there were terrorists coming during rush hour?!?!!) . . wouldn't it be an aspect of military funding??

Summer heat beats down upon the vast areas of black roofs and black pavements. Black is very heat-absorbent. Sometimes the heat is such that the tar or roofing compound softens, even bubbles.

But then it cools down.

What a waste!!!

Could there not be a grid of pipes atop the roofs, even fitted into slots cut in the parking lots and other pavements? Within the pipes would be a heat absorbing fluid that would convey the heat deep underground into chambers containing immense vats.

Stored heat!!! For later use when pumped into circulation for buildings close enough. Kind of the opposite of the old-days of cooling when ice would be cut from ponds and stored in extremely insulated buildings where it would stay frozen until the next winter. In the interim, it would be cut and distributed for various cooling purposes.

Back then, foot-thick walls filled with sawdust were at least one of the insulating "technologies". With our modern materials we should be able to create a "collaborating alternative" of actual ice for cooling along with compressor-driven "chillers" and other refrigeration for air conditioning etc.

So, too, with heating from what the sun had heated but we'd stored away. Another resource of waste heat is significantly in some nuclear waste. This is contained (supposedly) in absolute safety from any radiation leakage. The temperature of the containers is almost dangerously high, and will remain so for extended periods of months, at least.

Rather than bury this "heat-resource" out in the middle of nowhere's abandoned salt mines (now being done), shouldn't it be shipped to facilities where it could be used as heating? So these might have to be very secure, monitored, even shielded buildings.

But think of the jobs created building them. Hooking up circulating jacket piping around the hot containers, connecting same to heat-distribution systems analogous (and in collaboration with) the steam-from-generator-plants that now heat at least parts of most major cities.

A final thought regarding cooling. With sub-basement level origin, ducting up through the building distribution, and roof-suction-venting of air, so many buildings might be at least partially cooled just by air flow -- without air conditioning? And what if windows (or special, large openings) in commercial buildings could be opened? To let the breeze condition the air?

Re-usables and re-fillables.

Think the packaging. Think especially the plastic bottling.

Think, that even if recycled, the manufacturing energies and resources thereof are wasted when the object of such short "life" becomes something that has to be destructed to a certain state, then re-manufactured even using, hopefully, most of the remains of its previous incarnation (or in-carton-ation).

The carton could become analogous to the "pallet" upon which freight is transported. More and more pallets are specifically owned by pallet companies to whom they're returned after use. They're then re-leased (or whatever the arrangement) to the shipping outfits.

The same could be done to some extent with boxes. Cardboard might be replaced by some kind of plastic, essentially rectilinear shapes made slightly variant so the empty boxes could be nested for return to distribution centers from which they'd go out to subsequent shippers. Better if they could be folded down flat.

Massive amounts of essentially new (used just once) cardboard becomes recycled "waste", sent by the shipping container-full all the way across the seas for remanufacture in Asia. What a waste of the material and of the fuels to transport it globally.

Containers such as jugs should be refilled. The housewife goes to the store with her quart (or larger) container, deposits into the dispensing machine, and gets the detergent, bleach, perhaps even some edible liquid products.

Simply, collectively (and that's the appropriate term), if not refilled by the consumer, containers of all kinds should be . . . collected for re-distribution to be filled by the producer of the same or similar product.

Especially wasteful in my estimation are motor oil jugs, which are heavy plastic and actually "new". Pour out the oil and then they get not only thrown away but destroyed in the incinerator or buried in the landfill. Not even recycled!!

A combined container (boxes, bottles, jugs, and more) collection and re-distribution center would surely create a lot of jobs for the "low-end" wage-earner demographic. Considering that without such employment that group might have no alternative opportunity but to "collect", wouldn't it be better, even more economic, for the government to not only venture-capitalize, but, if necessary, ongoing subsidize this type of employment! Subsidize people earning money by preserving resources!

Those little tiny plastic water bottles . . . a couple sips of the Poland or Disani or whatever and they're empty and get tossed into the rubbish barrel and end up in the landfill. But they also become, "decomposed to and distributed as, molecular components" in the terrestrial and especially marine environment.

Bad enough that in over half the world the population (mostly the women) have to walk long distances to obtain impure if not dangerous water. In the "advanced" world we transport designer-doses of H_2O interstate and even trans-oceanic. And here and in other "advanced" nations, the local water supplies are not only pure, but monitored, and fluoridated to prevent tooth decay.

But we internationally ship water, sip the water from the little plastic demitasses which we then toss in the rubbish barrel.

The town of Concord, Mass (famous for the "shot heard 'round the world" and notable for its elite and affluent people) recently managed to pass an ordinance prohibiting the sale of bottled water in those little containers. I'm sure their perspicacity pervaded into other aspects of the water-waste such as I've mentioned above. But they could do something about this blatant waste of the container, at least. The precious free-market of plunder (resources for such transport) for profit (bottled water is expensive) itself was beyond even Concord's campaign to curtail.

But they got that ban on the bitty-bottles. Resulting in snickers and scoffs and even worse demean-ments from the right-wingers. Not just in the local paper, Concord's conservation ethic was subject to ridicule in national media.

The Concordians, I'm sure, took all this as an inverse adulation in that the deprecations of their accomplishment derived from the demonstrably dolt demographic.

At any rate, hardly a pittance of plastic saved *per bottlette*, but every little bit of conservation helps 'cause it all adds up. And the Concordians made a significant point to be pondered for those who are able. (Ponder is somewhat an exponential neural connectivity ability beyond prattle.)

And I pictured. . . . . .

Picture it with me . . . . .

"Welcome to Concord."

"I thank you. You've a fine town here, and famous."

"Yours the fame, sir, and fortune not to have been electrocuted!! But seriously, yes, we do have a heritage, and still the bridge." "Ah yes. The birth of our nation, one of the major birth pangs taking place right here."

"Well put, Mr. Fran. . . "

"Call me Ben. No need for such formality."

"Alright, Ben. Before I continue showing you around, perhaps you're thirsty."

"I could use a bit of quench."

"Right in here. This is our general store."

"The water barrel or dispenser?"

"Oh no, Ben. We got rid of such obsolescence long ago. We have individual portion containers. Here."

"So small, but the water looks quite clear. Hmmm . . . the glass feels pliable, soft."

“It’s ‘plastic’, Ben.”

“Amazing. Yes, this water is good. But so little in the container.”

“Here, have another.”

“Thanks. That’ll suffice, I think. Now where do I place these containers for further use?”

“Over there in that barrel.”

“It’s almost full with these containers already. When does someone come to refill them?”

“Oh, we stopped refilling things long ago. We just throw all containers away. Especially these little ones.”

“Throw them away? There’s nothing wrong with them!! Look, I even put the caps back on mine -- others have too -- why would anyone not preserve something . . . .”

“Not worth it. Too much trouble. We just dump them.”

“That seems terrible. UnAmerican. Ungodly.”

“But to make them is so cheap.”

“What’s cheap?”

“Oh, they’re each only worth about a penny.

And Ben Franklin realized the free-market driven economics of modernicity and proclaimed . . .

“A penny saved? That’s all? Hell, **WASTE ‘EM !!”**

DA BAIT (Mitt and Barack Debate #1)

It happened. But what was it?

When it was is clear. It was Wednesday, 9 EST on several stations.

TV stations, and probably the sound was broadcast on radio too.

First there was friendly handshake-greetings and male-bond-type mutual touchings of shoulders. Then the two candidates for the next Presidential term stood at their separate podia (or would it be podium -- "separate" denotes individual, singular: podium. But that doesn't sound right. Then how about "each stood at his separate podium"? Eh, who cares other than me!-I?)

Who else cares. The candidates' frequently overridden moderator, beyond and somewhat below their stage level almost like a "prompter" for a Shakespearian or operatic presentation . . . . was in his place. And the amount of time Mitt and Barack exceeded allocated durations despite attempted moderator interruptions and scoldings was pretty much equal.

Both parties of both Parties seemed respectful, almost congenial, and at times humorous inclusive of subtle self-deprecation.

No troublesome subjects were brought up or thrown (up to throw) at either of the . . . .contenders? . . . .

There was no mention of American Extremist Fundamentalist Phobias and paranoias: Mormonism being an a-Christian (if not, to some, anti-) cult. Not a word about Mormon Mitt.

There was no mention of the "flat-earther"-analogous fringe beliefs that Obama is an illegal alien (if not in his capacity of U. S. resident, in his position as President in that that specifies the occupant be of American birth. I'm sure there are some amongst some -- though not *us* -- who would attribute his proof of "citizenship/birth-cert." to Satan . . . . analogous to their asserting that anthropological fossils of "intermediate species" -- thus evidence of evolution -- were put where they were found by the devil.

As well as Obama cartoonified with a Hitler moustache, I've seen him depicted with diabolic horns and tail!! etc. in Internet stuff -- proof enough to some who know from other infallible (Biblical) source, too, that Beelzebub was not born in the United States of America.

There was hardly mention that the whole economic situation was the result of a "systemic pre-existing condition" and that at least Obama's administration has maintained a stability of (actually accomplished a slight ascent from) debacle.

There was scant mention of immigration, none of military guy-gays.

Both Mitt and Barack presented excellent appearance, admirable behavior, and constrained contexts of what they considered, thus what they . . . conversed about ?

There was no mention of gaffes such as Mitt's 48% or Barack's "clinging to guns and religion". Neither Mitt's "not concerned about the poor" nor Barack's "didn't do it yourself", both statements obviously taken out of context and expanded to *absurdum* almost as if issues.

No mention of Guantanamo, closing it the quest to revive Constitutionality (such as *habeas corpus* and due process). Too bad pervasive lack of hospitality resulted in no alternative venues in which to house the horrific (but as well, how many innocents just caught up in the chaos not wedded to it as actual terrorists, but sold to the coalition for some bribe-price to a tribal adversary?) That wasn't brought up as an Obama "broken promise" or "failure"

There was hardly personal *ad hominem.* Mitt could have mentioned Obama's "clinging-to-guns-and-Bibles" remark. Worse, about his inept bowling earning him a "Special Olympics score",or something to that effect. (Truly a thoughless analogy from the President of the country!! Various very pejorative critiques could be made of the reference: the "inferiors", relative to the referencer, Harvard unto Chief Executive, etc.). There was no mention of Romney's realm of almost obscene privilege (elevator for the car in one of the estates) -- the hardly proportionate-to-necessity "physical therapy equipment" for Mrs. Romney: $100,000 horse, dressage ring, stable, paddock, no doubt groom.

No mention.

No snide remarks.

No innuendo.

No taunts.

Not even put-downs.

Debate? More like a conversation took place on that stage last Wednesday at 9PM. A friendly conversation. There was no evident impatience, exasperation, annoyance, anger, and except for the few instances of humor (which both seemed to appreciate as humorous). Nothing really emotional took place.

Interruptions (futile to constrain running over time limits) and essentially ignored admonitions (from a mere PBS guy to the President and the multi-multi-millionaire) were made with self-effacing good humor too. The runnings-over were solely for a candidate to continue his statement to a necessary state of completion. Otherwise the "hanging-chat" (incomplete presentation of premise or policy) might function as "preemptive hanging chad" -- eventual votes lost due to incomplete information from candidate.

Except for perhaps two very brief incidences, I don't remember any overlap or attempted over-riding of "the floor". For the overwhelming most- part, Mitt completed his say, then Barrack had his, and vice versa. Little talking over, butting-in, gesticulating, gyrating. It seemed each was a respectful audience of the other.

The decision to have the audience itself remain silent, which it did (except for a couple instances of very subdued laughter), was wise. No "gallery gallimaufry" of sounds to .... de-dignify ... the .... *debate*??

If other than conversation, it truly seemed more like a presentation of projected policies (by Mitt) and review of achievements (by Barack). And these presentations were equivalent to what one would expect of very-upper level corporate officers presenting to the board as differentials, not adversaries.

But perhaps my perception of such professional and almost fraternal format was warped. Like, maybe, the on stage waters weren't as quiescent as it seemed to me. Maybe there was a factor such as when one witnesses a mere storm surge, it seems placid after he's been immersed in a veritable maelstrom for media-months, more like a tsunami of unending and unlimited reciprocal trashings, heard on the broadcasts of ballistics of bullshit of the campaign. In comparison, the stage- personal appearances were, relatively, pristine and poised. Yes, the term "dry" would apply.

But cordial, though maybe not quite convivial. . . . although seeing the co-mingling of Romneys and Obamas at the end, I wouldn't be surprised if they all headed off together for a great dinner and fine wine, then maybe to one of Mitt's mansions for an overnighter prior to their having to get on to their stumps and stances on the morrow. I can picture at least the younger of Mitt's boys challenging Barrack's girls on some video game while the parents perused, amused, the news reviews. (Though only one of the men uttered "whew!!"s).

For even in the PBS "playback" *immediately* after the event, along with the two women correspondents, the two men (one representing the NY Times, and I forget the older jowly guy's affiliation) opined that Mitt had "won". There was wonder if Barack was "rusty" from not having recently debated.

And I wondered if such, perhaps "catalyst" for other "grading-reportage" was actually a Democratic Party "strategy". Yes, I'm off in the conspiratorial deep end here. But from what I watched, "debate" didn't really fit. And the specifics, the components of "the debate" seemed almost ultimately removed from evaluative juxtaposition. And I'll move on to the next paragraphs to explain what I mean.

I'm not providing any extent of play-by-play here. I'm giving my overview and summary of what I saw and heard. A transcript of everything said would provide extensive examples of what I'll just touch on.

Barack "recited" his accomplishments, though without going into much detail. During his administration oil drilling, though below all-time highs, had increased. The unemployment rate, though still unacceptably high, had been brought down a bit. Institutions of crucial finance and manufacture were sustained (after Bush's initial "bail outs" as resuscitation). And there were several other areas that Barack presented as his administration's accomplishments.

Mitt by no means refuted, actually hardly challenged, any of the above.

I'm surprised that Obama didn't bring up the brought-up (to dangerously implosive levels in my estimation) -- the stock market during his term. **(Oh god, let's hope it wasn't because he knew enough not to wave *a bubble* as a banner).**

Yes, as well, both candidates stated several matters which resulted in disagreement unto denial.

One matter was that a Romney win would result in very unfair tax breaks/advantage for the very upper echelon. I don't recall that specific percentages or other statistics were given. Mitt denied that his campaign had ever said such a thing. It seems that at some point he stated, almost as a correction of misconception, that he advocated no tax breaks, but he would provide tax advantages in order to stimulate the economy/job-growth.

To this there was hardly rebuttal from Obama. "Break?" "Advantage?" Newspeak nuance??

An obverse concerned the effects of "Obamacare". Romney, without any details other than some agency "finding" (not his exact words) said that it would seriously and deleteriously increase health costs. Obama cited his side's "findings" that the result would be a significant savings for the lower income demographic, and, of course, expanded coverage for those who now have insufficient or no health insurance. Overall, Obamacare would save money.

Were it so simple, one or the other of the candidates was either basing information on misinformation, erroneous calculations, or conducting calculated misrepresentation of the actual financial-facts.

Obviously it's not so simple and, given the nature of statistics, both diametrically opposed extrapolations might be "true". Or neither. Or vice versa. But neither Mitt nor Barack pursued any depths of this area. That national health care had originated as a Republican platform issue was just touched by Barack. That Mitt had, (a state-level mini-mirror-image of the Obamacare resistance) managed to establish what I'd love to see called "Romney-care" as Massachusetts' government-regulated system . . . . was just mentioned, not "used" by Barack.

Both men seemed in agreement regarding improving education. Mitt asserted (more than once) that during his governorship Mass. schools had became the highest achieving in the nation. I don't have any notes to refute, but it seems that's not what I've read here or there. Obama did not even question Mitt's claim to high-scoring-scholastics fame.

To that point (rather, within the scope of considered contexts up to then), there seemed to be not a draw, but just a two-part presentation of their accomplishments (as President by Barack), and as governor (and businessman by Mitt).

A brief review up to this point:

Barack's presentation was to point out his accomplishments and his side's conclusions (though not evidence per se) concerning what a Romney administration would produce, entail, incur, but not unto *inflict*! Mitt's response was not a retort or refutation, let alone outright denial except for alleged amount of "tax break for the rich" regarding which he asserted, "I never said that". Barack let any contestation go except for a comment about Mitt now ("I never said that") not being the Mitt then who did say that. Wise strategy.

Focus on factuality (even questionable) puts anything personal in the periphery. Trying to nail Mitt on, (if it was) "denial" or "deviousness, might have been seen by the electorate as an attack-overcompensation for Obama's vulnerability!! Or as uppity-arrogance.

Another "persona-perspective" occurred to me concerning demeanors.

Dignity, even "somewhat stilted", is dignity compared to what a "loosened-up and 'got-down' " Barack Obama would personify in the racial-lens of so many. Even if not an actual performance, agile or argot, of the first "black" man to be President of the United States. Obama's white-ish presence was probably based on very careful considerations that any"blackishness" would be a serious blemish. Racism is regionally rampant still.

"Rusty from not having debated?" I return to that for a second.

Well, in a non-debate there was hardly opportunity for debate without (especially) someone being seen as arrogant, or elitist or controlling, . . . or out of his place. So, again, Obama was a polished presenter of his party's position, its assumption of accomplishments, and tactful, intended "factual" refutations of the other side's stance or statements in cases.

Yes, Barack was almost out-of-character controlled, staid. Compare to his speech at the Boston convention back almost four years ago. Compare to other presentations of his charisma, inspiring elocution. Compare to his campaign comments the day following the "debate" . . . . concerning Romney and the "wild-card" (not Obama's term) tax rebate/advantage amount for the uppers!!

As for Mitt?

To use the term, *"channeling",* may be an ultimate "concatenation of disjoint" -- meaning that such a "new-age" idea applied to right-wing Conservatism . . . might even be explosive -- or cause spontaneous dematerialization of concept! Lurid liberal times ultra-right equals zero?

But watching Mitt, smiling, energized, if not actually gesticulating (somewhat vertically brachiating), seeing his animation, amiability and all . . . . I couldn't help but wonder if he was actually *"channeling the Gipper"*. Either that or with coaches he'd been rehearsing his Reagan impersonation and got it down to subtle perfection more effective than anything more copy-cat blatant.

But maybe I just "saw-in", read-in "concatenation of similarity" (my extrapolated, or imagined, linkage but a systemic of epiphenomenal unrelateds).

Or something like that.

Focusing on Reagney (whoops, I mean Romney), can we deny having seen a transformation, a transmutation, a metamorphosis (from the wearying worm of so much editorial critique of his "dullness", etc.) . . . now this glorious flight (arms aquiver with enthusiasm) of the "better fly" (with him than with the "bumbling Beerack", Obama).

Reagan-routing or not, Mitt's animation, especially toward the conclusion of the affair, was effective, although it seemed to me a bit affected. Like, this isn't the "real Mitt". Kind of a Wendy's-ad thing, where it was almost like "good ol' Dave Thomas" chattin' (even after he lost so much weight he'd gained maybe eating so much of what his restaurants serve). "I'm-jus'-one-of-you-people-so-come-sit-with-me-at-my-table-Dave." From things I've read here or there, including a statement by one of his sons, it seems he was really a very hard-driven, hard-driving Type-A.

And all along for months, the Mitt seen on the stump-stops was not the Mitt seen on the stage where he pulled it off so admirably, animatedly. Behaviorally. I found myself thinking that Barack Obama appeared so "Waspish" . . .and Mitt was almost "grooving' to and with *his* rap." Though I don't think I discerned any actual cadence.

Other than regarding tax breaks/incentives(?) and a couple other "line-items", Barack really took no issue with what Mitt mooted. Again, they agreed on improving/enhancing education, Barack specifying his desire to hire 110,000 teachers (to pay with what? -- a question that Mitt didn't pursue.)

At the "contextual point of the 'debate' " I've reached in this discussion, I felt that equivalent validities of presentation and points thereof had taken place.

A TIE! if we're going to score a non-game, a non-contest.

For I didn't see it as a debate. If I spent the time to look up "debate" and compare all the facets and factors and components and complexities of this *"binary format of juxtaposition-for-evaluative-conclusion"* . . . . (wha . . okay, yes, that does make sense . . . .) if I really studied "debate", and compared, in detail and dynamic, what took place last Wednesday at 9 PM EST, I'm sure I'd be comparing apples to . . . . guys. Two men taking turns having their say. For there was no real juxtaposition, discreditation of data or declaration, etc. etc. etc. No rebuttals, retorts, refutations, retaliations, or the rest of repertoire that made debates of the past demi-dramatic demonstrations. This time it was simply declarations.

Two guys in suits on a stage behind podia (-ums?) before/above the "moderated moderator" from PBS (who I'm sure was careful because especially some one of Romney's companies might become a significant contributor to programming since federal funds to provide chamber music and opera to the teeming masses have been so drastically cut-off. (In my nano-contributory way, I make up for some of what the trusts and estates and corporations don't completely cover to keep the classics coming to me . . . while the curtailed Fed funding is allocated to *needs* such as health or housing perhaps. Access to the arts (such as classical music) provides for the *wants* of the "aestheticarchy" or "aestheticocracy", ***"artistocrats"***? Yet everyone can tune-in to listen or watch, if not attend cultural events. But it's somewhat an "elitist-minority" who are into what PBS provides. PBS should be private enterprise and private persons or other payments provide for it.

But I must not digress further, for it's getting late.

I'm not sure how far from being done with this diatribe/dissertation I am.

I really want to finish it tonight, for I have much reading to do tomorrow, some of which will no doubt cover areas on which I'm writing now, and which I may wish, thus, tomorrow, that I'd waited until tomorrow to write what I'm writing about rather than tonight. Eh, I can always insert text, can't I?

It's getting late.

I must be getting to . . . . . . where was I????

Da Bait. Yes. DA BAIT.

What the hell does that mean?

Well, on the one hand it's obvious that it's a play-on-spelling of "debate". But it's also a semi-homonym-ic transition of "debate" (discourse) to **"the bait"**, that which will attract and perhaps result in complete consumption of the candidate's presentation, (hook, line, and sinker) . . . by the voter.

Da Bait. The bait. That which at least gets the attention of the prospective catch, the voter. That which is cast upon the waters of the campaign, turgid, turbulent, or tastefully calm, really or relatively. Da Bait. That which may be swallowed whole by enough for the fisher of votes to mount unto the Washingtonian throne.

Obama's bait? It was his "this has been accomplished while I've been President. Like the configuration of a hook, here the focus turns "upon itself" as its field of consideration. Without refutation or dismissal by Mitt, one can assume that what Barack said was done . . . was done. And the "barb" of the hook of his bait may actually be that "*the American people*" are primary in his program of direct disbursements -- not the American Capitalists whose primacy, thus tax-related benefits, or perpetuation thereof, are supposed to result in jobs, thus payrolls, thus tax bases, thus government solvency, thus programs and progress for the masses (the perks of the masters totally above/beside the point). If not "channeling the Gipper", Mitt surely channeled "trickle down". He used a rather clever phrase, castigating Obama's alternative to Reaganian "trickle-down" (from private enterprise profit) . . . . "trickle-down government" as despicable, creeping-socialistic alternative.
(Mitt didn't allude to socialism, but I believe my words say what he would have.)

As for Mitt's bait?

His summation segment stated it in sequence of points he considered. Which I'm not replicating as a continuum here. But along with some of his points I will present my commentary.

Mitt stressed the importance of education, implying (at least) his role, if not responsibility/accomplishment, in elevating the level of Mass. schools.

> But I don't remember his detailing any federal program to thus enhance the <u>nation's</u> schools other than providing from Fed $ to the individual states to administer and distribute to schools.

He acceded to the importance of health, care and costs, improvement and control, respectively.

> But his promulgation is, again, a state-administration, provided with Fed funding. Mass's "Romneycare" is a state system. Mitt somewhat chided Barack for "forcing" Obamacare via "unfair uni-partisanship" -- as opposed to Mitt's supposed "crossing the aisle" for bipartisan enactment. That Mitt cited some supposed "confraternity" between Tip O'Neil and Ronald Regan involved, stirred a bit of mirth from the commentators. It seems that between Tip and Gip there was no love lost (how Fed funding approval for the "Big Dig" was forced thru Congress is fascinating . . and had stirred Reagan's comment, "I haven't seen so much lard since I judged a prize pig contest at a Kansas fair" (apprx. words).

Mitt noted being in favor of developing alternative energies.

His one "semi-*ad-hominem"* concerned the off-shoring of Evergreen Solar, the bankruptcy of Solyndra, and mention of a couple others. Mitt's mention that Osama's "investments" were into losers was "debatish" but, more, devious. And Obama's non-rebuttal, though perhaps strategized, might have lost points he'd have scored had he pointed out that 1) the very bastions of business and industry had either departed our shores or defaulted thereon . . .and 2) Mitt's contention -- that Fed$ Obama had put into these failed alternatives ventures could have financed pay for X# of teachers . . . is in a sense a senseless nonsequitor. Any attempt finance alternative energy is valid.

That we invest in alternatives is of strategic importance unless we just don't give a crap about our great-grandchildren and beyond. That some of those start-ups don't survive may reveal more the faulty Fed Govt. (compared to other countries as in Europe (surely not just China) where subsidies support experimentation and development of alternative energies until they hopefully become self-sustaining, even profitable).

Mitt mentioned clean coal. He's in favor of that as a major energy resource. Great for the very minor constituency who mine (or strip) coal. Great for assuring their votes.

But what about the environment, including atmosphere, in the couple generations(?) duration until the seams' and decapitated mountains' yield run out?? But coal is bait for coal miners. And mine owners. Yet how small the employment-demographic, thus voter numbers.

Another matter in Mitt's bait-shop -- oil drilling. Flat out he stated he favors drilling in Alaska and on the continental shelves. More than bi-part bait here. For one thing, oil companies and personnel must have been instantly hooked hearing that proclamation.

And this gets me into several sub-areas of concern,.

First, just how many unemployed people does Mitt think he'll get back working by providing for more drilling, on- or off-shore? How many run a rig? I should look it up so as to cite data, but it's already a bit later than when I mentioned it getting late before. So let me "guesstimate". 500 total involvement per rig? So let me venture that we could put into pumperation a thousand rigs. That would give jobs to 500,000 people. Out of how many millions (+/- 8% of the population now unemployed . . . . .!?!?!?)

Second, I'll just mention the potentials for disaster. Each rig may represent (as a respected friend of mine stated it) a "small footprint". But as I replied unto him, citing Valdez and the little burbling miss-hap by BP, petro-drilling footprints sometimes bleed profusely!!

Third, who in his right mind would expect that more oil pumped out of anywhere is going to lower gas prices here (or anywhere) to @$2 per gallon?

If one has adequate information (which I have but smatterings of) he realizes that it's almost that the oil companies are governments unto themselves. And their prices and profits are surely not "consumer-driven" (supply and demand) -- for they can diminish their supply (due to increased automotive efficiency or decreased consumption of product due to mobile curtailment -- people traveling less) and maintain "windfall profits" just by pumping-up pump prices! ExxonMobil and the others don't only have a cushion to protect them from any and all of anything . . . . they have a trampoline!!!

Fourth, As for OPEC, our "dependence" on their oil is far from threatening. From Canada come our primary petro-imports. And regarding OPEC itself, if we suddenly said, "screw you guys, we're outta here", how long would it be before those swarms of Saudi princes would be smothered by insurrection, and in the brutality of The Brotherhood or Alqaida or Martyrs or myriad other jihadis who would thus be unleashed from the West's militari-economic tethers of restraint? Our proxy-princes . .

Fifth, petro-input from wherever isn't always allocated to specific distribution. It seems there's kind of a "global pool" drawing from Africa, America, Canada, Caribbean, Chile, Norway, Mideast, Russia, Venezuela, and many elsewheres.

One example of the "dispersion" is that, from what I understand, the majority of oil we pump out of America gets exported!!! Via the "collective pool".

Sixth. Does it really make sense to exploit our proven reserves (of anything -- even, or especially, if it lowers consumer prices) in order to stimulate even more usage of an ultimately finite resource? Even with the expense of trial-and-error (invest-but fail) interim of economic allocations, isn't R&D toward functional alternatives (especially "self-sustaining" such as solar, wind, wave) preferable to diminishing what we have but is non-replenishing??

It seems, without actual statistical analysis, that there would be far more jobs created in creating completely new systems, than those few people put back to work on oil platforms, mining or fracking facilities, etc. And if, in a few generations, the US, in part thanks to Mitt, has depleted its "conventional" (oil/gas) resources, what then?? Perhaps we'll be so much less dependent upon "foreign energy" sources when we have none left? Would the neo-OPEC with headquarters in Sharia City extend philanthropic pipelines and shipping lanes from their shores to ours? Would the energy cartels of any country then say unto America, "you tried so hard, you conserved so much, your people went without . . . . how can we now help you out with a somewhat Marshall-plan-ish provision of what we've preserved???

Still sixth: employment opportunities will result from new devices, systems, installations, not just the alternative energy sources. It would seem that Federal investment would be in such as priority.

Wind-solar and later other sources to supply LED lighting via even separate building circuits (though interfaceable with the conventional Grid).

Collection of and separate plumbing systems to recycle "gray-water" for non-potable use (such as for toilets, industrial processes, etc. Knowing that water supplies are in drastic decrease (factoring population increment and deglaciation) . . . . to use pristine H2O in which to piss and shit is . . . . unconscionable!! (Also consider that we can ship Coke and Pepsi etc. all over the globe but millions have limited access to any water, and most of it unsafe!!

On-site housing (condos on office-park-campus expanses, even on all those acres of flat roofs), would not only put an awful lot of people to work (who wouldn't want to or be able to work on the oil rigs -- which wouldn't be able to employ them all anyway) . . . . . . and think of the commuting time and fuel consumption and pollution spew

saved if one's commute to work would be but a
few minutes' walk!!! (How well I know!!!) .
Instead of the daily miles and miles of creeping-hour (rush?)
migration.

Yes, I could keep on going with categories of innovation and thus, as well as ecological benefit (or salvation), broad economic advantage even beyond job creation.

But enough. I hope I've made my point.

I felt that Mitt Romney's points were far from prodigious. Rather, they missed the points of what priorities should (and will have to) be. Except that as "bait", they were excellent. Mantras. Slogans. Drill, baby!! Petro-self-sufficiency!! Good ol' coal (so almost nostalgic). Domestic energy!!

One of Mitt's summation points was, "We can't keep going on the path we're on (referring to what Obama has really had no choice but to tread as his itinerary despite his best intentions.)

But Mitt's bait is based on everything, substantive and systemic, on which the errant and error'd path already taken has led us to -- where we're at!! *Laissez-faire* of the free-marketeers (business-boom based on credit/thus-deficit), banks bundling debt as if collateral compounding, overseeing agencies as ratings-sellers charging top price for the triple A. We've traveled that free-market path. States' rights as God's grounds for determinations -- thus such despicable disparates as health care, education, prison conditions, capital punishment criteria and on and on. You got Vermont and you got Alabama and you got Texas . . . . . . states . . . . deciding . . . allocating . . .

Obama's bait? His presentation of what he's accomplished against the "odds" of the outcomes of the gambles (and worse) of an administrations-continuum from before (inclusive of the S&Ls, the Greenspan bubble, the ongoing interim legacy costs overwhelming product-mediocrity of Detroit, the eventual outcome and realization of what seemed to Wall Street (global-"Wall Street") a profit bonanza of "securitizations" -- (the new "tulip" of profits).

Could Obama *have* done, could he do better? Better?

I think one of his statements was salient, concerning superseding partisanship regarding Obamacare. He said something to the effect that sometimes to lead, one has to just overcome by assertion (and, implied, even manipulation). But given "gridlock" there was only so much possible. And thus the protections of our government's "balances and checks" can result in . . . . checkmates??

Would Mitt do better? Mitt's proposals, his bait, will hook some. But they may find they're swimming the same submerged path which brought us to where we're at.

Other than oil and coal, where will all those jobs come from?

He stated he was sick of paying money to China (apprx. words). Does he really think that it's a matter of China sucking off our economy -- which is our major manufacturing & marketing corporations!! (Walmart, for just one egregious example) so significantly profiting by doing business with/in China??. Even heavy, heavy industry profiting the US interests, dividends?

Doesn't he realize to what extent China's cheap labor is "an inverse input into *our* domestic economy" via that upper level demographic known as shareholders? Doesn't he realize to what extent American investment is in "Chinese" enterprise -- somewhat analogous to the "Japanese takeover" back some, what, 20 or more years ago? The Japs even bought Rockefeller Plaza!! Remember? Aghast, some bewailed and berated our "sellout". At exorbitant prices. Resulting in windfall profits for the sellers and even eventual re-possession of the defaulted and foreclosed properties when that market bubble busted and the Japs lost much for which they'd overpaid much.

Nobody's selling-out our own economic interests to China. We're exploiting China's economic interests.

But Mitt must have managed already to antagonize that massive, major populace and its leaders, prospering partner with us in globalism, but potential enemy if the "détente of economic symbiosis" were severed.

Will Mitt's bait actually provide any nutrient to those hooked? Not just, I might term it, "notion-nodules upon which to nibble?"

Ah, but perhaps the solution, the evolution of it all . . . . .
somewhat as the conclusion of projected-policy-presentation . . . . .
Mitt really enthused, "we'll get that pipeline built" . . . .

next

The V.P. Debate

Will it be, "better a Biden"
Or would you rather a Ryan?

or would the most mastery be by Martha?

Was it her "her-ness"? Female . . .

Such long hair and other features of her younger, probably exquisite beauty . . . still radiant . . .though matured.

So was it (too?) a "mother-image"? rather than just some old guy even positioned "beneath" Mitt and Barack. Last night this glowing, mature woman was on the same plane as (perhaps even higher *level* than) the guys in the VP show.

Though there were several instances of Ryan and Biden (especially the latter) interrupting, even persisting beyond his allotment while the other had begun his turn, even in these cases (of, I felt, childish impolitesse), it seemed she was in control -- allowing a little tussling, so to speak, but quite effectively putting a stop to it when she'd decided "enough too much" was enough.

Striking appearance: those high cheekbones somewhat suggesting "facial *broad shoulders*", thus strength, even power . . . . Was it by her "Valkyrie"-ness that Martha was able to curtail and control both the contestants so well? (In the third of the four-opera series *The Ring Cycle*, Brunhilde is the name of the leader of the Valkyries, the warrior women of the god, Wotan).

Martha Raddatz. The Brunhilde of the debate? For me to conflate her in any way with a Germanic, especially Wagnerian, character, may seem a juxtaposition far worse than the "*channeling the Gipper*" comment in my "Da Bait" essay. By the last name, I would assume Martha is Jewish. "German", in juxtaposition!?!?! . . . . especially when we bring in Richard Wagner who was one of the first to propound Jewish as ethnic. The Jew was no longer deficient and despicable due to the religion. It was his very *being* by heritage and "race". Thus, no longer possible was the "assimilation and salvation by Christian conversion. Jewish had become an incurable, unconvertible blood disease. There could be no "transfusion". Just, soon, *transport* due to Wagner's philosophy influential to Hitler's hate, not just the music to love.

Some time ago on some TV history thing I saw footage of Wagner's great nieces (?) and other relatives along on some outing or parade with him, and one holding Der Fuehrer's arm.

But to the debate.

Regarding Mr. Biden.

He made several semi-errors with facts and figures, words and terms. Most he caught and corrected immediately, including one comment involving the word "devastating" which his initial sentence seemed to be applying to the US's effect upon some situation abroad -- rather than the existing "devastating" situation itself -- which the US was attempting to resolve or ameliorate. I don't remember the specifics.

Biden's "ideational flow" had an interesting, somewhat distracting, pattern: the last word of a sentence would be, so to speak, over-ridden by the first word of his following sentence. The effect was "an abbreviation of terminal word" of a sentence, the meaning and intent of which was complete (at least in Joe's mind). So he thought no need for a "coda-word", so to speak -- a word after his stated completion of his thought. And so he'd get on with the next component of thought or thesis, the next sentence.

Interesting pattern. Usually this happens *between* people, one "coming-in" to dialogue as an overlap, a preemption of the other's completion. Biden's bipart barge-in is self-administered!

But I didn't find it deleterious to his, apparently, genuinely personal statements, actions, and interactions. This "spontaneity" spanned a spectrum from just looking and listening rather intently, to actions and reactions such as "what a bunch of crap!!! (he used the word 'baloney')". He laughed, almost scoffed now and then.

At times he became vehement, agitated, almost angry in response to Ryan. In these instances, it would appear that Biden was retorting with factual, documented, standpoints and information such as military chiefs-of-staff approval of, if not initial advocation of, Afghanistan draw-down -- also "ally" accord with US on deadline date. And there were a couple other issues.

Biden's grins, grimaces, and smiles, at times seemed almost, if not Tourettish, at least inappropriate, maybe silly, maybe supercilious. And there were at least two occasions when he protested to Martha that his opponent was having (especially for closing statement, might have) more time than he'd get. He sounded almost adolescent, bitching. Petulant.

Mr. Ryan's presentation was less interrupted by "instant self-corrections". But he, too, caught himself on fact or figure, a few times.

In significant contrast to Biden, Ryan's persona was a smooth, somewhat flattened continuum. My impression was that I was hearing and watching a meticulously rehearsed recitation and performance. Precise, and practiced. A speech -- without the spontaneity of statements (and certainly emotional and behavioral emanations) of Biden. No improvisation from Ryan.

The issue of foreign nations' loss of respect for America almost seemed a refrain, a *leitmotif,* played in several context-themes: failure to be more involved in Syria, not supporting Israel/Netanyahu sufficiently, proposed cuts to military. (I'll return to these matters below).

As with the Presidential debate, here in VP-land there were the stalemates.

R) Obamacare will cost billions and be deleterious.

D) Obamacare will save billions and be advantageous.

D) Enhancing, even just maintaining, tax cuts to the "rich" hurts the middle class & economy itself.

R) There will be no tax cuts, rather "relief" for the upper levels and this will allow investment into the economy to create jobs and help the middle class.

R) Raising business tax level will devastate small business owners, forcing them to close businesses.

D) Almost no small businesses owners make over $200,000 per year, thus the overwhelming majority of "business" will be unaffected by tax increase on the rich.

R) Cutting military budget will weaken America in the estimation of others

D) Military expenditure is excessive, in part going to provision of redundant or excessive (example given was tanks) equipment.

And there were a few other cases where the two sides were just contrary standpoints without any in-depth, or -breadth, examinations of situations and circumstances, documentation, data.

So, again on the VP level interaction, it was rather than a debate, it was more an "I say it's this way", "but I say that way", reciprocation of antitheticals really with no basis other than "platform" premise. No even purported *proof* within historical or contemporary context for the efficacy or wisdom of premises and platform positions.

Concerning what I said above that I'd return to . . . . .a number of concerns.

As above, R) is obviously for Republican premise, D) for Democrat.

1) Iran's nuclear program.

SANCTIONS

R) sanctions haven't stopped Iran enriching U, etc. Obama policy reveals weakness to stop Iraq's threat to develop nuclear bomb.

D) sanctions are working and will eventually force the Mullahs to supersede militaristic ambitions in order to sustain their theocratic positions from eventual popular insurrection (obviously my words here for what Biden was presenting as the Administration's rationale and assumption that basis its sanction policy).

There was no "rebuttal question" to Ryan such as, "had Romney been President, what would he have done heretofore. **Specify**. If Romney is elected, what will he do, assuming that Iran's actions and intents will not be altered just because of an administration change in Washington. **Specify**. What steps would a Romney presidency take, what actions? Criticizing Obama's alleged ineffectuality is far from a statement of intent, plan, platform.

The Obama administration's steps and actions are obvious -- existing policies and procedures. *De facto,* so to speak, if not by universal international acceptance of their validity, by overwhelming majority of concerned nations, the present paradigm is deemed the wisest course of action -- no preemptive military action, even to (try to) destroy Iran's facilities (a la Saddam's back some time ago). And it seems that if Israel decided to do so as last resort or preemptive self-defense, it would go ahead even in actual abrogation of its agreements, and violation of relationship, with US. What, pray tell, would the US do about it? Disown Israel? The West Bank building boom should be seen as an example of Israel doing what it will do regardless!

The threat of igniting the *whole* Middle East by "a fuse of fusillade" (so to speak) vs. Iran was cited by Biden, with references. Would greater respect for, perhaps fear of, the US be engendered by staging a "second act of Iraq", but this time not with an outcast outlaw (the semi-secular Saddam, hardly aligned with, rather, primarily despised by, his contiguous nations)? Would Islam-extremist rage (and retaliation) be rendered less threatening?

Perhaps especially to Israel?? Stuck there in the middle . . . of potential suicide-bomber *populations*?

I see Iran, or any other, unlikely to become a "suicide bomber <u>nation</u>." No doubt there's full awareness that if it did launch anything serious against Israel, Iran would be "obliterated" by the retaliation of a large coalition. Iran isn't hard to locate -- whereas terrorist *individuals* are just that, without populations and agendas and factions and financial enterprises and amassing of wealth and interests in survival for themselves, their families, their investments, and all.

A preemptive attack on Iran would, of course, be judged as primarily Israel's action (though US backed). How much greater the rage, thus individual terrorism the more stirred to wipe the Israel off the map if it actually enacted destruction on Iran!!! How "contained" and "confined" in source and system is Israel's water supply (for example). How much greater the existential threat to the country and its people . . . . after preemption on Iran . . . thus unknown, unmonitorable individuals with little vials of virals in their attache cases . . . or even shoved up undiscoverable places of person as they perused Tel Aviv before pouring into its pipes.

Perhaps some of these considerations should have been brought out by Biden?

But if time constrained, again, should he not have cornered Ryan by demanding, "Just what would a Romney administration have done to this point? And what will it do if elected?? SPECIFY!!!!!!"

One of Biden's points with brief but comprehensive backing information concerned Iran's stage with enrichment, vs. when it might have a weapon in which to put the stuff. Ryan didn't contest Biden's references. But Ryan should have picked up on the "no where near having a weapon". What happens if nothing happens to change the escalation, now just enriching? Somewhat a convoluted analogy to using up our resources until . . . WHAT NOW . . seemed Biden's post-ponement of concern about Iran developing a nuclear weapon for its nuclear fuel. Maybe a bit of a ways off. But time passes. And . . .WHAT THEN???

Ryan should have ordered, "Specify!! What then -- *whenever*?"

WITHDRAWAL

R) Obama policy of set-date withdrawal from Afghanistan gives notice to Alqaeda so they have time to prepare for re-takeover/re-insurgency.
(this obviously an approximation of Ryan's statement).

D) Withdrawal date set not by US alone, and provides time frame (and necessity's incentive) for Afghan troops we've trained for that purpose to take over responsibility for their own country.

Biden did mention that to draw down such a theater as Afghanistan requires extensive time and logistics and coordination, so can hardly be contained until a "we're out of here, bye!" surprise.

And he could have further figured even if secrecy were attempted, leaks are unpreventable. The populace not being told in advance, thus "weaned" through a period of time, might see the US and allies as betrayers, devious, sneaks, and worse than even the other opinions they seem to have of us.

There were no considerations of whether our persistence is really defeating its very premise -- our attempted "advanced" democratization and modernization thus catalyzing the proportionate resistance by the very "socio-status" of the region (tribal, theocratic, misogynistic, and worse, to us -- but to them their valid reality).

Prior to Russia there were other lost-causes for some Western interests. Less under the guise of free-the-Iraqi-people "idealism" (our shtick) in *their* intention to secure routing of Mideast petro resources, Russia's actions in the area led to their withdrawal (by thwart, if not actual defeat).

US presence as an invasion, even defilement, of the Muslim realm is proliferated in public's perspective (propounded unto the populace from the pulpits of the Mosques). Another Crusade. An attempt to crush Islam -- as well as to superimpose (what we think of as progress and modernicity) our <u>decadent</u> immorality and materialism (which they, like our not-too-long-ago-Puritan-and-other-persuasion-forebears would, consider the sins of the Satanic!!)

Again, what would Romney have, or what will he do differently? SPECIFY!!

INVOLVEMENTS

R) Obama has not sufficiently provided support to overthrow Assad. Weakness revealed by Russia and UN superseding US unilateralism (so to speak) to enforce its national strength, accomplish its goals.

D) US has been acting within international contexts (again so to speak).

A President is not a dictator, either domestically or internationally. Within our system there are divisions of power, provision of checks and balances, veto, over-ride thereof. In very few cases can a President *Constitutionally* act alone. A final "contrarian decision" by

Truman, to approve a Middle East Jewish state, defied the unanimous dissent of his whole cabinet. But even in this case there was the preceding "infrastructural" Congressional involvement.

Another situation was with the Bush/Cheney (and neo-con) con -- of Congress and others. This was a matter of mis-information (unto outright bullshit) by Bush and his little bunch. It led us into a multi-morass, billions debt serious, but insignificant compared to the loss of life, infliction of such suffering upon so many who managed to stay alive during the neo-"siege of Baghdad". And what, pray tell, was accomplished to strengthen our country, enhance the world's opinion of us, let alone others' *respect*?? We not only lost lives, we lost face!!

And prior, though we were justified in driving the Alqaeda-sheltering Taliban from power post 9/11 (we asked, and they could have turned Osama over), our continued involvement in Afghanistan accomplished what? At the cost of so many lives, for us to drive the militants out of their caves in the wilds of Afghanistan? Accomplished? There, logistics for their re-supplies were quite difficult for them. Communications, though, were very easy for us to monitor. But we cleansed them out, displacing them, no doubt, into the cities of Pakistan where vis-à-vis (no cell phones necessary) they could plot their plans and order their arms and huff their hookas totally unsurveilled!!

Our expunging the militants from the mountains of Afghanistan seems, to me, to have accomplished about as much as . . . . if during the roaring twenties the FBI had gone into the realms of Upstate New York and driven all the gangsters out of their getaways and conclaves. And when they'd all been "flushed" from the forests into the big cities of New York and Chicago, the Feds rejoiced, "We've solved the Mob Problem".

Regarding other areas of "involvements" . . . cases of sheer imposition by a nation, including ours, (without "weakened capacities" incurred by contexts and constraints such as UN, NATO, whatever) . . . . .

With Bush (*pere*) as head of CIA (and, interestingly, Kermit Roosevelt as primary operative and the father of Desert Storm Fame General Schwartzkopf in a major role, we surely got involved in Iran, overthrowing Mossadegh in order to reinstate the Shah (and Western control of interim-nationalized petroleum industry). And look what that led to rather soon. Hostages. Repressive religiosity. And the Iran of now!!!

How 'bout the "Arab Spring"? Western intervention primarily as incentive, approbation, cheering-on, maybe some weaponry, even a little air support . . . it seems that the overthrow of Libya's and Egypt's (like Iraq's) corrupt and cruel leaders has resulted in an expanded region and rule of "United Islam", truly A Brotherhood (and other titles of the factions/sects/divisions of the militants. And these represent a dispersion of direction now beyond our control.

The volatile vapor of a militant confraternity-unto-populace is a far worse threat than a contained pool of family or fanatic individuality, in spite of the corruption, even to some extent the cruelty. For let loose the rabid hordes, does not the carnage and cruelty just increase?? At least we could manipulate Khadafy, Mubarak, et. al.

It seems that the Romney-Ryan position is almost as criminally naïve as was the Bush-Cheney catastrophe regarding democratization of the Middle East through "controlled demolition of despotisms" -- Saddam as the fuse to set-off the regional chain reaction).

Regarding the regressive, repressive Saudis, what would Romney do? In ways, Saudi Arabia and its rulers represents a far worse scenario than many other places and personages. Think women's non-rights as just one example, Saudi Arabia in juxtaposition to, say, Turkey or even Iran!!! Wahhabism. Saudi support of terrorist organizations. Saudi origin of all but one of the 9/11 team. Etc.

It seemed that Biden should have nailed Ryan. What would Romney do?? SPECIFY!! About Assad? SPECIFY!!!! Make Syria and Iran the second of a double header firsted by Iraq??

Maybe that's the answer to the problems.

HAHAHAHAHAHA WIPEOUT!!!!

Scorched-earth policy. Neo-blitz firestorm finale of the whole wretched realm of regression and religion. Biblical!! With high-tech. Every man, woman, child, beast, and poison the fields to be ever-after barren.

And horrendous consequences, including that the enactment thereof would reveal the enactor as exponentially worse than those expunged by the explosives.

Would "regional genocide" be an ultimate Romney route? (Mormons for Armageddon?)

SPECIFY!!!!!

Iraq recent history

After WW II, America turned to the Middle East for petroleum supply. We established ally relationships with Saudi Arabia and also Iraq in order to secure our sources.

1987 Revolution in Iraq which turned toward Russia, also became anti-Israel. Us cools relationship and deals with Iran (overthrowing Iranian govt. which had nationalized their oil industry . .and we reinstated the Shah).

Iranian fundamentalist Islamic revolution. Our hostages taken and held for over a year. West realizes that Iraq not so bad as Iran.

1982 Iraq prepares for massive invasion of Iran . . springboard for a larger effort to thwart Iran's springboard of Islamic fundamentalism into other areas of the Middle East. American policy makers argue that Saddam is no different from other dictators American had worked with through the years. Iraq must be a defense against Iran.

America sides with Iraq. From 1982 through 1990, the U. S. policy is that "the enemy of my enemy is my friend". Reagan administration removes Iraq from its list of terrorist nations. So doing aids the
U. S. in supplying Iraq in its war with Iran (but we also supplied Iran with all kinds of strategic materials and weaponry and intelligence!!)

1983 Regan sends envoy to "make nice" with Iraq: Donald Rumsfeld. This was after the U. S. knew of Iraq's use of the U. N. banned mustard gas in the war. The U. S. State Dept. condemned Iraq's actions but took no punitive action.

1983 Reagan renewed actual diplomatic ties with Iraq the first time in two decades. After this, American support for Iraq increased -- involving critical information on Iranian troop movements. Agricultural credits were provided to Iraq to buy food from the U. S. so money could be allocated to the purchase of weapons from us. The extent of the agricultural economic-involvement was such that there was much lobbying for the maintenance of Iraq's approved status and recipiency.

Washington loosened control on the export of weapons and encouraged allies to do the same and "look the other way" when necessary. So all kinds of weaponry was sent to Iraq, thus contributing to the development of the "weapons of mass destruction" (which, before Gulf, Iraq possessed with our blessings). The U. S. contributions included selling Iraq strains of anthrax.

1987 campaign against the Kurds, many of whom had allied with Iran during war. Iraq uses poison gas. Indications of attempted genocide: 100,000 killed.

1988 U. S. Senate passes bill to punish Iraq. House waters bill down. Reagan administration kills it. Economic reasons are primary. In addition to the oil consideration, Iraq was the 2nd largest buyer of American agricultural products (second to Mexico).

1990 Iraq invades Kuwait. U. S. launches "Desert Storm", defeats Iraq in the desert, but also bombs Baghdad.

2003 Second Iraq war. Stated reason: to disarm weapons of mass destruction.

Misc. information regarding Saddam

His father died when he was a young boy,. He was sent to live with a relative who was abusive, and his interaction with neighborhood children was such that he was harassed as a "bastard".

Saddam lived with another relative in Tikrit. The person had been in prison for an attempted anti-British coup. Also, here Saddam was influenced by a culture of familial and tribal values which were the core of society and identification of the individual as well.

early 1950s Saddam demonstrating against rich land owners.

1958 revolution overthrows British backed monarchy

1959 Saddam and Baathist fail in attempt to assassinate the Iraqi military leader. Saddam flees the country for four years.

1968 Saddam has returned and risen to power in Baath Party. Takes over security division, eliminates his rivals. On the basis of "Arab oil for the Arabs", money is put into schools, infrastructure, highways, etc. Lives of people are greatly enhanced. Baghdad becomes a cosmopolitan city.

1979 Saddam takes over presidency of Iraq. Videotaped purge of "traitors". Saddam on stage smoking cigar as supposed traitors' names are called out and they are led out, many to be killed.

1980 invasion of Iran ostensibly over a territory dispute concerning a waterway, and also due tot the Iranian fundamentalist revolution which Iraq (and the Western powers) wanted to keep from spreading. The eight-year Iran war killed more than a million people. The West supported Saddam against Iran.

1981 Iraq nuclear facility bombed by Israel. Saddam had stated, "The Iranian people should not fear the Iraq nuclear reactor . . .not meant to be used against Iran . . . .but against the Zionist enemy."

1988 end or Iran war. Billions of dollars of Iraq debts, Saddam wants cancelled.

1990 Iraq invades Kuwait, blaming West for stealing Iraqi oil (angle drilling)

1991 Saddam forced out of Kuwait. Baghdad bombed. Reported pinpoint accuracy of U. S. patriot missiles. Extensive looting by populace should have been precedent for what has happened now. But the only protection seems to have been given to the oil ministry building . . .while the mobs stole and destroyed everything else and U. S. military did nothing.

Brief history of Iran

1906 A constitutional revolution had taken place but was suppressed by the monarch, Ali Shah.
1907 Actual control of Iran was essentially divided between Britain and Russia
1908 Oil finally struck after numerous unproductive drillings
1909 Largest refinery in the world built at Abadan on Persian Gulf
1911 By then, pipelines were transporting oil out of Iran under the control of Anglo-Persian Oil Company
British executives and other personnel lived in luxury
Iranian laborers subjected to horrendous saqualor
1920 Iranian royalty accepts British terms of 16% of net profits of Anglo Persian Co (per an.), amounting to just L47,000 for one year.

Worldwide depression ensues and oil revenues decrease, thus royalties to Iran fall.

(As is now in the Middle east, notably Arabia, the "pittance" payment from Western oil extraction entities represented great luxury for the royalty and high-end few. But there was next to nothing of benefit to the common masses.)

Social and economic conditions in Iran resulted in cancellation of the oil concession to Britain. . . thus the necessity of Britain's renegotiating the agreement up to L975,000 per an. and decreasing the size of the concession lands.

1941 Britain forces Reza Shah (the ruler responsible for the above) to abdicate
1945 Between '41 and '45, oil extracted increases from 6 ½ to 16 ½ mil. tons.
1948 Active in former nationalist movement but forced into exile by Shah for 20 years, Mossadegh elected to Majlis (like our Senate)
1950 Mossadegh became prime minister of Iran and was trying to negotiate a 50/50 split of oil revenues with Britain
Britain absolutely intransigent in refusal
Mossadegh ultimately inflexible in compromise.

Mossadegh nationalizes Iranian oil industry and expels all British personnel. Britain sabotages Iranian Oil operations

Refuses visas for technicians answering ads for Iranian oil industry positions and pressures other countries to do so

U. S. and Britain own 2/3 of world's oil tankers. Britain influences and U. S. refuses any Iranian shipment of oil

Ship *Mary Rose* transporting Iranian nationalized oil seized by Britain.
Iranian exports of $45 million in '50 close to zero by '55

Prior Truman administration would not cooperate with Britain's colonialist intentions regarding Iran. But Eisenhower came into office and went along with Churchill's agenda providing U. S. (SSA renamed CIA) with authorization to overthrow Mossadegh and reinstate the West-friendly Shah.

Coup against Mossadegh organized under George H. W. Bush's leadership of CIA. Primary operative organizing mobs and handing] out money in Iran was Kermit Roosevelt. Also Schwarzkopf's dad.

7 D

The cause of war . . . .

. . . . the locus is the leaders . . . *

The invasion of Iraq was the conception of and inception by a determinant little power clique, in this case termed an "administration". Other times and places, "monarchy", "holy Roman Empire", "sultanate", "junta", and other names have applied. By any name, in any case, this is how the world has and still does work: the unholy trinity of sheer power, religious imposition, and wealth/resource acquisition per se or through economic control of their markets. There is always an admixture of these conquest condiments, and though there may be a *focus*, (an emperor, *fuhrer*, tsar, comrade", pope, or other), such "lead man" is guided or influenced or coerced or even the outright puppet of his "intimates" and "advisors" . . . . who are generally the true representatives of the wealth and power of fief or kingdom or empire and now even hemisphere.

The immediate cast of the tragi-comedy of the present is a triumvirate of stars (Bush, Cheney, Rumsfeld), and two major supporting actors (Rice and Powell) the latter reciting and acting-out the worst bad-drama concoction of the major three.

War can be declared and simply imposed, so to speak. An empire or dictatorship has a "victim-population", the military establishment essentially an enslavement at least of the young males. From quick-death to its imposition through various durations and duress of heinously creative means (crucifixion through firing squad or life imprisonment at hard labor), populations of places and times have had no choice but to wage war for the whims of the power-elite. There can be no allowance for pacifism, etc.

But an element of war and those who fight derives from basic male human nature, it seems. Almost instinctual aggression is like an "endo-regime" so often. And some hyper-aggressive personality, thence some assemblage resulting in a quorum of intentions, and small-scale wars are almost like spontaneous aspects of psycho-social interaction. In some primitive societies, micro-warring (raids) are the *raison d'etre*.

And it is this dimension of the human that, even latent in times of peace and preoccupation with living and loving . . . . can be coerced or stirred by government and the thousands will lay down their tools and take up the offered arms and march off somehow "lemming-like" to drown in the blood of slaughter. Crusades. . the almost sportsman-like motivation to join the game of death, destruction, mutilation and disease (the plagues contracted by the few able to return home, thus to infect those at home after so doing to those along the way). Civil War.

Of course, a major factor leading to war and leading those called the warriors, is Information. Also collusion, distortion, outright lies, defamations are the components of *brainwash*. "Truth" and even "rationality", even to sophisticates and intelligentsia, can be but functions of directed propaganda or factors of media bombardment and immersion (such as what American publications and at least the Economist (English) provided us starting mid-2002 and proclaiming to us at least up to the "end" of the Iraq war.

* This, written in c. 2002, as part of my "Iraq Debacle", the "leaders" to whom it refers could easily be [illegible]!

Another consideration of our present situation and its ramifications is that even now when we'd assume (or have been led to believe) that compassion, conscience, and even common sense would be the right and freedom for the individual to act upon, come the orders to ship out, there's hardly a choice. As recently as the "refuseniks", prosecution and incarceration would result. Prior, dodgers were jailed and deserters shot. And a bit priorer in the land of the free, I've read that Irish immigrants essentially "impressed" into the Union army were branded on their foreheads for trying to desert the suffering and carnage.

One might assume that "in this day and age" in America, all such would be behind us in history. . . . or elsewhere from us in realms of regimes or African rampages. For our democratic system is tripartite, each checking and balancing the others.
For our well-established government has, in addition, a bipart *legislative* branch elected by the people. Said branch must approve of any war in which the country will engage. And although this process obviously is not a popular-election (per se) of war-stance (for or against), it is "representative", supposedly, of the population's wishes.

There is intended implicit concensus and a comprehensive basis thereof. Ethics, opinions, beliefs, theories, even plain manias and mongerings (representing the various opinions of people) are meant to form a "data-base" by which a Presidential/military agenda and even its "intelligence" are to be evaluated.

The breadth of man's ideations distilled in the democratic institution of elected representatives' expertise and insider-involvement should . . yield the elixir of perspicacity and wisdom and thus be synergic of the "majority-merit" when a vote is taken and the checks and balances of democracy ensure truth and justice to all.

HAH !!

There are flaws inherent in this beatifically-intended system.
We have so clearly seen them during Afghanistan and especially the Iraq debaqle.
"Redefinition" (Orwell's "newspeak"?). Exaggeration and mere conjecture can be termed "Intelligence." Honesty (such as about the Iraq-Africa nuclear info in the speech) is a non-issue where "our best intelligence at the time" is the cover or there's an underling on which to pin blame for careless editing or something.
The power of the Presidency and behind the government is mega-business (military-industrial-petroleum complex). The top politicians (administration) wear their public personas like masks over their actual corporate faces.

Accountability and even constitutionality can simply be evaded by "executive edict" with the pseudonym of National Security. For example, the military can hold someone without legal aid up to , apparently, indefinitely . . . . and a military tribunal usurps the role of judicial process (court trial).

I don't think I need to continue.. This little dissertation seems sufficient as introduction to my final segment on Iraq. And certainly the material in the prior sections may adequately present a span of consideration . . . .including the veracity and validity of my editorial and philosophic promulgations . . . . . or not.

So let me simply say that I hope the following pages provide a sort of overview and review of what I've covered before. . . . . . . and maybe the images and ideas for some profound introspection about where we're at, where others are, and what such disparities may mean for our homeland security.

Big Iraq Attack!!!

. . . . looks like we found the weapons of mass destruction after all. They looted and burned and now bomb and escalate their attacks and what's next . . . . . .

The most destructive weapons are deprived and enraged people in so many nations in the world . . . .

. . . . . and now in another newly ravaged place. . . . .

Is our "War on Terrorism" but gasoline on the white-heat of rage?

MILITARY

We surely need to maintain a significant conventional armamentarium: land, air and sea things from hand-held to bombers and refuelers, tanks and trucks, and guns and gear, and floating things up to carriers carrying thousands.

We need "boots" in training and at-the-ready active.

Even slight chance of some provocation by or confrontation with China (or North Korea) is sufficient reason that we keep competently conventional.

However, 9/11 should suffice as a premise upon which to base the protocols of our preparedness!! The proportionate potentials. Hardly a chance of a foreign country coming at us with any sort of military force. Why would they waste the effort? Money? Isn't it rich? Isn't it rare? No need for ships on the sea or planes in the air. So where are the arms? There have to be explosives. They'll send in the suicidals!

The size of the US military budget, at $472 billion, is higher than that of the next 17 major nations combined and 3 times more than China. For what purpose other than defensive status? As offensive force, the offense to others has been far more pervasive in their hatred of us for invading, destroying, maiming, killing -- than any shock and awe supremacy of our prowess or the hardware of shock and awe. All the billions accomplished what, other than disruption and destruction, in Iraq? Afghanistan? And much of the world's opinion of us.

Have we become (the opposite of the "mouse that . . ") rather, "the dinosaur that roared", rattling our monster-military sabers while the viruses of extremism and terrorism (and even ecological entities) represent far more insidious and potentially invasive detriment to us -- even unto our destruction/extinction?? (A guy with a vial from regions Tigris or Nile. . . . .awaiting the right moment by . . the water supply.)

A book I obtained awhile back was titled *Killed Cartoons.* The cartoons had been submitted to, but rejected by, The New Yorker. One of them showed two stick-like figures plummeting downward beside the smoke-billowing, sketch- representation of one of the Trade Center towers. The caption read, "If only we'd had a missile defense system . . . "

Terrorism is the major threat to this and other countries (this was acknowledged by Ryan). Against terrorists, conventional weapons are the equivalent of dynamite as deterrent of cockroaches or termites. What good would Star Wars have been against the attack by in**tra**-continental ballistic missiles bearing passengers along with their fuel tanks of mass destruction??

From the British back in the 1700s to the Russians in Afghanistan to the Americans in Iraq, a fighting "force" is almost a futility of formulation and formation when confronting the dispersion of an insurgency or terrorist network even called Patriots.

An article I have mentions the Army's request to stop production of M1 tanks (42 of them for $255 million!! divides to apprx. $6,071,429 each). Despite un-need, the appropriation for their manufacture was approved. Another, the F-35 Strike Fighter ($200 million per plane) "described as 'mixed' performance" is being considered for cancellation -- but it seems the issue is not military necessity, strategic importance for our nation's strength in the eyes of its foreign beholders, even efficacy or need of the whatever . . . . but a matter of how many jobs will be lost!!! How much MIC corporate profit cancelled.

Considering "sequestration", the projection is that it "would cost more than 1 million jobs by the end of 2013 and 'The impact on industry would be devastating,' said Robert Stevens, CEO of defense giant Lockheed Martin. He told congress that his company, which received 82 percent of its revenues from the government in 2011, might be forced to furlough 10,000 of its 120,000 employees if the [D] cuts go ahead.

Here, such an interesting glimpse into the hypocrisy of R protestations against government programs being but socialistic schemes in government-subsidies'- clothing. There's been no Romney comment to the effect that we've got to bring down the deficit no matter what and if it hurts the MIC (military-industrial-complex), let market forces be and the companies succumb (a la suggestion for Detroit and banks). Above quotations and data from "The Week", October 2, 2012.

On the following pages a list of the R-proposed non-military cuts. The webside-source is noted.

Somehow, somewhat obverse to the seemingly socialistic mega-subsidy of the M.I.C. by the government (talk about "pork" -- $6+ million dollar per tank even though the army already has more almost than it has room to store)! I was saying, somehow, somewhat obverse is that these "civilian" Romney cuts almost seem to eviscerate the very organism of America as a society and culture, collaborator with its collective constituents, and colleague with other nations in some respects.

Such clear-cut harvesting of our evolved notion (and implementation) of national greatness! -- to provide for the semi-obsolete paradigm of military excess, both of material and manpower -- almost seems a treasonous attempt to subvert our *democracy*'s distribution for the fulfillment of the peoples' pursuit of happiness . . . and establish a "*militocracy*" A military nation. One nation under M.I.C.!!

Eisenhower . . hear him rolling over . . . mumbling . . . "they didn't listen . . .. "

Romney tax cuts, website source obvious on first page following.

9A

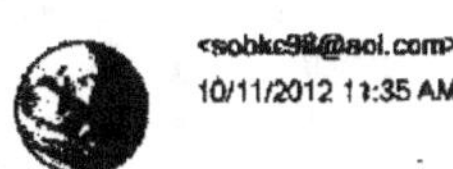

<sobkc98@aol.com>
10/11/2012 11:35 AM

To <RMegan@nemf.com>
cc
bcc
Subject Fwd: List of Republican cuts in Ryan's plan

Hi
Thought it was worth reading
Bob

-----Original Message-----
From: etmurad <etmurad@comcast.net>
Sent: Thu, Oct 11, 2012 8:00 am
Subject: Fwd: List of Republican cuts in Ryan's plan

Subject: List of Republican cuts in Ryan's plan

List of Republican cuts. Clearly, Paul Ryan knows how to make the cuts necessary to get this country back on track.

<u>Notice S.S.. and the military are NOT on this list</u>

These are all the programs that the new Republican House has prop to the end and pass it on to as many as you can.

* Corporation for Public Broadcasting Subsidy -- $445 million annual sa
* Save America 's Treasures Program -- $25 million annual savings.
* International Fund for Ireland -- $17 million annual savings.
* Legal Services Corporation -- $420 million annual savings.
* National Endowment for the Arts -- $167.5 million annual savings.
* National Endowment for the Humanities -- $167.5 million annual savi
* Hope VI Program -- $250 million annual savings.
* Amtrak Subsidies -- $1.565 billion annual savings.
* Eliminate duplicating education programs -- H.R. 2274 (in last Congre

McKeon, eliminates 68 at a savings of $1.3 billion annually.
* U.S. Trade Development Agency -- $55 million annual savings.
* Woodrow Wilson Center Subsidy -- $20 million annual savings.
* Cut in half funding for congressional printing and binding -- $47 milli
* John C. Stennis Center Subsidy -- $430,000 annual savings.
* Community Development Fund -- $4.5 billion annual savings.
* Heritage Area Grants and Statutory Aid -- $24 million annual savings.
* Cut Federal Travel Budget in Half -- $7.5 billion annual savings
* Trim Federal Vehicle Budget by 20% -- $600 million annual savings.
* Essential Air Service -- $150 million annual savings.
* Technology Innovation Program -- $70 million annual savings.
* Manufacturing Extension Partnership (MEP) Program -- $125 million
* Department of Energy Grants to States for Weatherization -- $530 mil
* Beach Replenishment -- $95 million annual savings.
* New Starts Transit -- $2 billion annual savings.
* Exchange Programs for Alaska Natives, Native Hawaiians, and Their
Partners in Massachusetts -- $9 million annual savings
* Intercity and High Speed Rail Grants -- $2.5 billion annual savings.
* Title X Family Planning -- $318 million annual savings.
* Appalachian Regional Commission -- $76 million annual savings.
* Economic Development Administration -- $293 million annual saving
* Programs under the National and Community Services Act -- $1.15 bil
* Applied Research at Department of Energy -- $1.27 billion annual sav
* Freedom CAR and Fuel Partnership -- $200 million annual savings.
* Energy Star Program -- $52 million annual savings.
* Economic Assistance to Egypt -- $250 million annually.
* U.S. Agency for International Development -- $1.39 billion annual sav
* General Assistance to District of Columbia -- $210 million annual savi
* Subsidy for Washington Metropolitan Area Transit Authority -- $150
savings.

9c

* Presidential Campaign Fund -- $775 million savings over ten years.
* No funding for federal office space acquisition -- $864 million annual
* End prohibitions on competitive sourcing of government services.
* Repeal the Davis-Bacon Act -- More than $1 billion annually.
* IRS Direct Deposit: Require the IRS to deposit fees for some services processing payment plans for taxpayers) to the Treasury, instead of allo part of its budget -- $1.8 billion savings over ten years.
* Require collection of unpaid taxes by federal employees -- $1 billion t **<u>THE HELL IS THIS ABOUT?</u>**
* Prohibit taxpayer funded union activities by federal employees -- $1.2 ten years.
* Sell excess federal properties the government does not make use of -- savings.
* Eliminate death gratuity for Members of Congress.***<u>WHAT???</u>***
* Eliminate Mohair Subsidies -- $1 million annual savings.
* Eliminate taxpayer subsidies to the United Nations Intergovernmental Change -- $12.5 million annual savings ***<u>WELL ISN'T THAT SPECIAL</u>***
* Eliminate Market Access Program -- $200 million annual savings.
* USDA Sugar Program -- $14 million annual savings.
* Subsidy to Organization for Economic Co-operation and Development million annual savings.
* Eliminate the National Organic Certification Cost-Share Program -- $ savings.
* Eliminate fund for Obamacare administrative costs -- $900 million sav
* Ready to Learn TV Program -- $27 million savings..***<u>WHY?????</u>***
* HUD Ph.D. Program.
* Deficit Reduction Check-Off Act.
* **TOTAL SAVINGS: $2.5 Trillion over Ten Years**

My question is, what is all this doing in the budget in the first place?

CIVILIAN CUTS

So these cuts would bring down the national debt . . .and "get this country back on track"? Toward a continuing recession (at least). For what would all the people dis-employed from these agencies and institutions do? Work on oil rigs? What would all those depending on the programs do? Hold up cardboard signs at street intersections because there are no more jobs on oil rigs? Or as senior citizens or disableds they couldn't get hired anywhere?

The Romney/Ryan proposal is to provide $Xtrillion in "tax relief" to restart the economy? Talk about throwing money down drains. What happened to the $X-whatever the amount was of the Bush tax breaks, proportionately highest to the most wealthy? Didn't see many jobs created! Rather, that prod to prosperity was just another push toward the plummet we're still close to the bottom of.

Tax relief. Uncut military bloatget (bloated budget). But he's going to create millions of jobs? Doing what? It would seem that unless military expenditure were increased, putting more people to work involving military manufacture or activity would not be possible without lowering wages of those now so employed, thus to share with the new influx!!

Maybe a Romney administration would issue executive order to Walmart and Apple and Gap/Old Navy and Conair and all the rest of once-America's employers . . . "This is your new President speaking. You must now return your manufacturing/assembling to your homeland and pay American wages to American workers." Or would it be, "Come on back and we'll make sure you don't have to pay your American workforce any more than you're paying your Chinese and Vietnamese and Bangladeshis and Indians and Madagascarians and South Koreans and god knows I've seen boxes (especially of clothing) with names of origin countries that I've never heard of!!! To make so much stuff that gets sold and old (and usually long before) thus ends up disposed of in such quantities that the agencies are overwhelmed and the fabric gets demoted to "rag-stock" and baled and shipped back across the seas to be made into carpet under padding and other conversion crap. (see following pages). . . . . .

There was just superficial mention of the myriad jobs Mitt will create?

Biden's reaction was like a teenager listening to the make-a-believe world-changing plans of an adolescent (which, at times, seemed Ryan's demeanor). Biden seemed amusedly disgusted, even "aghasted".

He should have demanded, "What will these jobs be? GIVE ME SPECIFICS!!!"

MEDICAL

Regarding Obamacare -- again, the stalemate of does it work and save, or not and cost. Will it benefit the populace at the expense of businesses which have to be able to pay people other aspects of "populace-benefit" (wages) -- which Obama-care costs will siphon off? Will it usurp choice? Deny services?

Ryan stated that "bureaucrats with no medical credentials" would be making decisions about medical procedures under Obama's plan. Rather a stretching, or convoluting, of the situation. This "panel" or whatever it's called, would be making decisions, but not actual medical ones. That approval of "elective" procedures might be within their domain of decision? Isn't that already the situation where insurance-o-crats make decisions concerning approval of coverage for this and that, and far from just pre-existing conditions and outright elective surgeries etc.? How many even health- (if not even life-) -involving procedures are denied coverage? And how many of those insurance company personnel have medical credentials?

A thought came to me as I heard this rather brief bit of the debate.

Having private enterprise insurance companies determining coverage, thus payment, thus often attainability of medical procedures, is not unlike foxes in charge of chicken coops. So too, sometimes, the pharmaceutical companies are predators in purportedly protective positions. Thus the need for FDA.

But regarding Obamacare, Biden stated that the AMA was in favor of the program (or most aspects of it under consideration in the debate at the moment).

Ryan didn't dispute or refute that.

ABORTION

So contentious a subject.

So contradictory the concept that the death of a mother and an unborn child (for example because of a drunken driver or a shooter), constitutes double homicide -- but the unborn "life" can be taken (within time-frame) as "maternal-domain decision" regarding her body's "reproductive rights-determination".

But that "reproductive-residency-requirement" (of at least maternal acquiescence) pervades *life*, almost as a female prerogative (as producer of life, <u>or</u> <u>not</u>). Some animal species (rabbits, for example) will "reabsorb" embryos, even fetuses, given deleterious circumstances of the environment. Some will devour their offspring, a sort of post-facto abortion from reproductive . . . into "recycled" consumption into digestive . . . . system!! Many other animal species, both male and female, commit consumptive infanticide.

Humans through the eons have proactively aborted and post-facto-ly "exposed" (or worse) the unborn and/or unwanted. There came to be for the born but not wanted, such "family-surrogate" institutions as work-houses, orphanages, and so much worse, such as purposely crippled beggar children kept like slaves.

The present parameters of *sanctity of life* seem to include a segment of time and cellular proliferation from conception until birth. The furor over stem cells, which would be disposed of, being used in research perhaps to heal or regenerate fully born, even adult-with-kids sufferers of diseases or dystrophies and such, seems hypocritical, or split-brained.

To preserve the sanctity of the unborn justifies killings of abortion practitioners?? Quite a distortion of “an eye for an eye” to “a sentient human being for a systemically pre-conscious cellular cluster“. If the sanctity of soul exists in the just-conceived, it would follow that it exists in the ongoing-organism incarnation unto an adult person. If that adult’s beliefs or actions are “sinful” (such as abortion), to commit on him (murder) what he is accused of (abortion) is but compound-crime-commission.

Even the non-violent vehement commit a sin of omission, in my estimation.

So many people with so much time to stand with their signs and their anguish that there might not be another brought into the world to, “diffusely-de facto” deprive one already alive and wracked with malnutrition, disease, and swaddled in the post-partum amnion of its own body‘s spews . . . while fanned by the flies..

What about the sanctity of the sentient, the sensing, THE BORN????

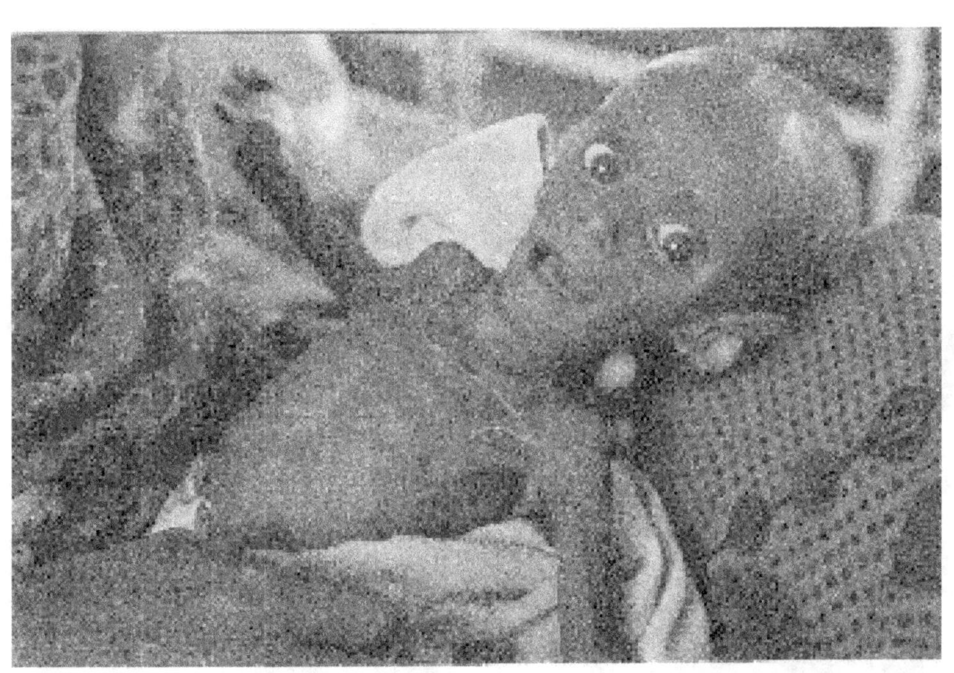

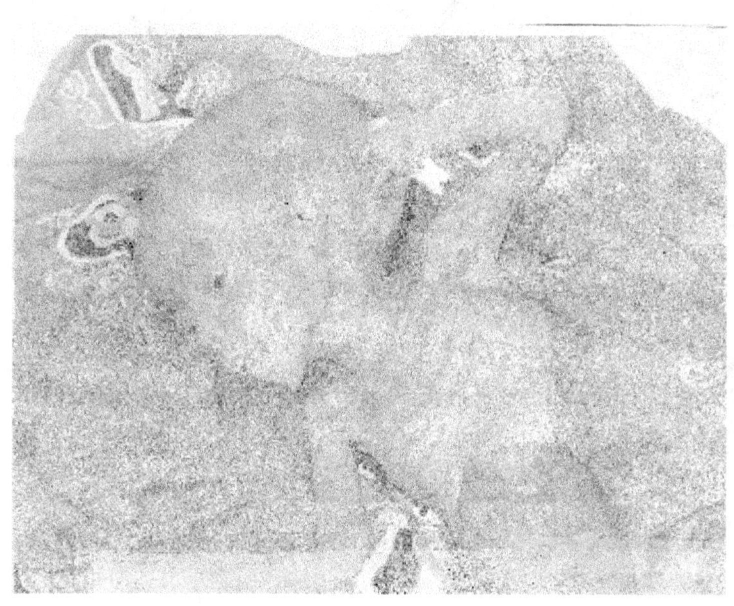

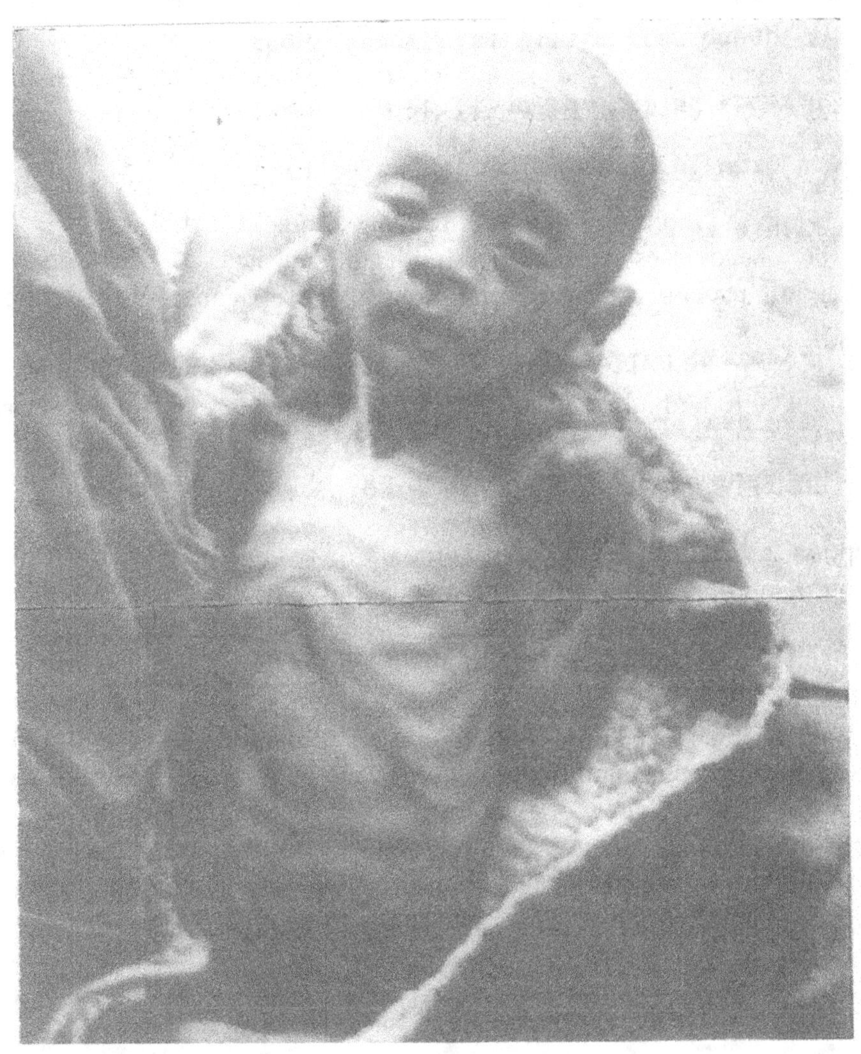

3 yrs. old

The impact of the photos above caused me to almost spontaneously sob. And there are thousands who thus suffer and waste while the "sanctity of life" is so protested and protected here by well-fed (if not fattened) self-congratulants congregated on the curb!!!.

What about the born? The starving infants?

Where are the protesters? Where are the Evangelicals? Where are the right-to-lifers when so many of the **born** so searingly suffer . . . and die . . . .slowly . . . while the signs are shaken and the voices shout and in the time they're so engaged perhaps they should, instead, be holding up pictures such as these (instead of abortion photos) and collecting money from passers-by to send to some food agency to keep the living alive -- rather than clamoring for the mass production of more sacred lives while others suffer and die.

Or live and join the thousands of AIDS-orphaned kids? What about their "sanctity of life" -- before they become psychotic killers under the auspices of The Lord's Liberation Army . . . mere training to become barbarian hordes when Alqaeda sets up shop in Africa and really gets them organized. . . . .

The sacredness of life? Rather, the self-sacrament of "caring" for that which the protesters don't have to be bothered with, especially touch. Especially those dark-skinned ones. NOMCO (not of my concern). Let "free-market forces", *business,* deal with life that has already been born, hopefully ambitious enough to stand on its own two feet. The unborn can't.

If conception is life in the same *existential status* as post-partum life, why not posit that conception is but a combination of the actual, *essential* constituents thereof -- sperm and egg. In former times, to ejaculate without a potential pregnancy receptacle thereof (woman) was held to be a sin. Onan's sin seems to have been as much *disobeying* his order to screw whomever it was, as his "spilling his seed" upon the ground. But the order to screw implied that the "seed" was the substance of life. Heaven forbid if male masturbation again becomes tantamount to "componential abortion". For how long would it take to get to *menstruation as murder* de facto? -- and all about Eve (and all females at least of some Simian species up into humans) the worst sin will be seen as this spilling of egg(s) (along with the endometrial nest??)

Pardon, I've let myself get a bit carried away.

Biden and Ryan, both acknowledged Catholics, acceded to the Church's anti-abortion stance. Both were succinct and clear. Ryan would allow for contingencies such as rape, life of mother. Otherwise Catholic doctrine would be platform, policy. Biden adhered to his Catholic faith, but excepted those with different beliefs. He did not feel that the government should impose religious conditions or constraints. The US government should not, so to speak, be the proxy of the Vatican and legislate imposition of Catholicism upon people of other faiths or non-faith, even in the area of abortion.

Thus, Biden was implying the continuation of present abortion policies and precedents (RvW), and trimester durations for termination.

To the question of Roe V. Wade that began this segment of the debate . . . perhaps Ryan should have been cornered. "Be Specific!! Would a Romney administration attempt to overturn Roe?

To the question of Roe V. Wade that began the segment . . perhaps Ryan's noticeable hesitation before responding. . . hid . . . thus revealed . . . his answer . . . . . .

CONCLUSION

Consensus represents *actuality*, an ever-fluctuating, variability. Social. Ethical. Political. Economic actuality. "Where it's at". The dynamic of the society and its component systems (government and private, social and scientific, religious and secular, etc.) is "the actuality". It's what is. Individual prejudices and predilections and philosophies and beliefs become subordinate to the eventual "composite" actuality. The process-outcome of group supersedes the individual preferences of guys and gals, straights and gays, rights-to and freedom-ofs, and all the other diversities of humankind.

This reality, "actuality", doesn't mean the individual should be subordinated, subjected without recourse. And we have established a pervasive recourse system in the "free-world" as our systemic actuality. The group as after-all determinant is a consensus, the summation of individuals (even via such computational contortions as the Electoral College). People vote. Contentions, compiled and computed, form consensus/majority which becomes formalized as "legislation" and "law". And extrapolated even from absolute antitheses of standpoints, beliefs, even expertise and perspicacity, comes the consensus spokesman.

The guy who wins the election.

Great system. It works. Even by its not working!! in that it encompasses a "governor" by means of parliamentary procedures, even those which can result in "gridlock". Better that than run-away, rampant factional impositions. Thus the protection from the extremes unto fanaticisms. Sometimes such result from consensus segments unrestrained. And the non-consenting can become victims when consensus becomes radicalized, or otherwise skewed. (Think the Sunni and Shiite shit). Think communism in China. Think Taliban.

I think we're safe from such threat. But even should a clique-consensus-surge result, say, in repealing Roe, there's that ultimate over-ride/veto/undermine/ of rule and even law and regulation -- human nature.

Back to the back alleys. Or perhaps a market for research into quite simple do-it-yourself potions soon available on the black market. The realm of drugs (drug-drugs) is a prime example of such pervasions or dispersions that law and order can't shut down.

So too was Prohibition

FINALLY TO SUMMARY

An Obama win may mean another term of only creeping recovery. For the very economic system *in toto* seems to have became a Ponzi process of making more jobs to pay more wages to provide for more purchases requiring more production requiring more wages to pay . . .(drained by such extensive off shoring of jobs). And this "economic eddy" has been further diluted and dissipated by an incremental out-flow into the containers of billionaires and millionaires and the gold-lined cloud-chambers of the 1+ percent. Evaporation? From the vortex?

It may only have been on the basis of inflated real estate values as a "debt-collateral standard" (not a gold-standard "substantive" . . which, itself is obviously not a bedrock considering the inflation of gold/per/ounce along with other precious metals). Prosperity based on irrationally inflated real estate values, transmogrified into indebtedness (mortages), "bundled" and sold as securities (collateral debt) . . . . talk about an (at first inadvertent, but later concerted private sector) betting BLUFF!!!!!

Another consideration.

The President is represented and deprecated as a sole determinant, so to speak. The Presidency is "anthropomorphized". The President is "characterized", even as Satan (or Hitler). But he's the spokesman/"fronts-man", for the vast group of advisors and specialists which comprise the administration. Yes, in cases such as Truman's on Israel and Bush/Cheney with Iraq, determination or deviousness can divert scrutiny and screw the systemic political, legislative, bipartisan (etc.) process. But generally the government represents a kind of consensus itself.

Among Obama's advisors there are such people as Warren Buffet, hardly an incompetent regarding economics, business acumen, investment strategies, his billionaire-level far surpassing Mr. Romney's mere millions.

In spite of the idealistic and ritualistic recitation by Ryan, Mr. Romney would be facing a consensus situation not all that different from Obama. To try to implement the list of cuts (on the pages above) would bring his administration up against drastic push-back from those whose interests and dividends and wages are paid by such programs. Also by those who personally depend on the programs for survival.

Again, how many jobs would be lost by such flaying of America's fabric of societal-security . . . in order to maintain the fool-metal-jacket uniform of military superfluity?

An Obama win, -- a continuum of a significantly same scenario as the last 4 years.

A Romney regime? The direction of the political game's gridlock would just reverse. D blocking R attempts at forward-passings of platform proposals. Of late it's been the reverse. A Rommey win would probably be a case of what the rock group, "The Who", so perceptively stated as concluding lyrics of their . . . "we're marching in the streets . . . ." song.

"Here's to the new boss, same as the old boss".

The Third Debate in brief.

Obama, as in the previous encounters, presented his administration's accomplishments, acknowledging that the economic problems have not been satisfactorily resolved, sufficient numbers of unemployed not put back to work. He noted there have been modest improvement in those areas from when he took office.

He mentioned the draw-down from Afghanistan, the withdrawal from Iraq, amending, in response to Romney's criticism, that the procedures are being carried out in collaboration and cooperation with the Joint Chiefs.

Concerning the Middle East, Iran and Syria specifically, Barack stressed that his policies are not unilateral, but represent a sort of consensus of many *concerned* nations (at the least, some *contiguous* to the turmoils).

Regarding Israel and Netanyahu, he denied turning his back on Israel in any way. More than once he stressed that we would stand by Israel.

In all areas, it seemed to me that Obama presented a reality, an actuality, of ongoing domestic and international dynamics. To some extent, or in some ways, either a degree of improvement, resolution, or at least removal has been accomplished or is in the process. For other matters, immediate resolution may not be possible. Especially in that those Mid-East matters are in the Middle East, for the U. S. to align itself with the interests (and possible survival) of those in the region is, itself, an accomplishment of multi-national policy. Even restraint as strength.

It seemed that Romney's presentation, as in previous appearances, was . . . promises, promises, promises. What he perceives as US weakness he'll strengthen by not letting others' interests supervene our own, our nation's prowess. For if others see us as weak we're in danger from them. He has no realization that, at least since Iraq, our "North Korea-ish" militaristic threats would be scoffed at best, beset by terrorist-backlash at worst.

His statements regarding Israel could have been read from the same policy prompter as Obama's. Israel is, of course, not only our responsibility in humanitarian dimension. Israel is our proxy military force right there in the midst of the mayhem Mid East. And Israel's protection is also the provision of votes and contributions from the significantly important (and well-off) Jewish-American-Zionist Diaspora.

Regarding military and might, Obama cited the statistic that the U.S. spends more than the next 10 nations [it's actually the next 15] put together, and three times more than China's. His position is that some of the military budget goes to redundant, unrequested, even unwanted materiel or equipment (such as tanks).

Romney's cited statistic concerned some type of naval vessel, and that we now have fewer than quite some years ago.

Barack countered that we now have far fewer horses (I think that was his example) than we used to. (The Boston Herald termed this Barack's "Snark-attack" on Romney"). Times and strategies and technologies have changed. We now have stealth jets and aircraft carriers etc. etc. He implied (if not documented) that the type of ship Mitt mentioned was, if not obsolete, unnecessary for our defense, even in modern offensive warfare's paradigm.

Again, the math. miasma: Mitt's tax relief yet debt reduction yet military-spending retention doesn't figure. Yes it does. Barack's economic policies (especially Obamacare) will bankrupt the country if not the people too. No they won't. Each had some survey or analysis to cite for corroboration.

On a couple occasions Mitt, looking almost hurt (and I wondered if this was strategy to gain sympathy) . . Mitt complained that

Obama was attacking him personally. The "attacks" (rather, critiques) were on Romney's proposals, his platform -- and it seemed quite a missed opportunity that Obama didn't quite pointedly point that out.

And also, that if contesting opposing stance comprises a personal attack, then Mitt had comMitted far worse by criticizing almost everything about Barack's policies, including that he only invests in "losers" (Solyndra, Evergreen, renewables, etc.).

Mitt's proclamation of prowess was that he'd successfully and bipartisanly conducted his term as governor of Mass (again, he stressed, the while, getting through a highly controversial state healthcare program not drastically different --given state-to-nation-proportions -- than Obamacare -- by "working across the isle. He also noted his accomplishments, his success, as a businessman.

Here, another missed rebuttal by Obama, I thought. In running a business one does not encounter a system of inherent checks and balances on CEO position. One may deal with some "politics" and even connivance, but "partisanship" is hardly a level of bifurcation of the operation of a corporation!!

In conclusion, Barack reiterated what has been done during his tenure.

And Mitt made more . . promises, promises . . . he's going to stimulate the economy -- going to put 15 million Americans back to work -- going cut programs that are sucking out of the economy and inflating the deficit, the first to be Obamacare -- going to get that pipeline built and make America energy independent

> and why didn't Obama, here, point out that the
> pipeline would be bringing in shale oil from
> our present biggest supplier, Canada?

. . . Mitt's going to get private enterprise back to where it feels safe to invest in American businesses and employment

> and why didn't Obama, here, point out that
> it's the government that would be (as has been)
> paying the private sector corporations that are
> involved in the making of military matters.

I heard a pervasive deprecation of a presidency that has not been able to get us out of the predicament that the proposed platform of its replacement would pursue as continuum of that of the administration prior to the present one!!!!

And you can unravel that last paragraph -- and see where it's at and where it'll be, depending on who gets elected.

The Fallacy of Free-Market Individualism

"Should" or "ought to" don't function here.

Yes, taking on a debt, be it a mortgage or otherwise, one *should* accurately calculate what he can afford to pay. The party *ought* to be responsible enough to not overextend herself. If a couple, they ought to, they should, be in charge of the private enterprise of their private "business" -- their income-to-expense balance even in projections of variables and viscissitudes.

Free-Market Individualism's standpoint would be that the actual locus of culpability for any economic crisis is . . . the people. their failure of "should-ing" and "ought to-ing".

These, the people of the general populace, I'll term "the former".

"The people" of the highest echelons of finance (institutions, raters thereof, regulators of both and beyond) . . . . these people "should" have and "ought to" have been not only responsible . . . . but given the mathematical formulas and hierarchy ("quants" etc.), synergized (or **sin**-ergized) by computerized computations -- these "people" were educated experts.

These, the people of the economics echelon, I'll term "the latter".

"The former" were computing their transactions not from some bygone era's simplistic notion of "common sense". For even back pre-credit days, "common sense" as the thought-function-default of the common-person would most likely be revealed as either an oxymoron . . . . or a *de-facto* status of not having leeway to exercise their common senselessness (such as a debt-based consumption of products and services has revealed -- which didn't exist back then in pre-credit days).

"The latter were, though, computing their transactions within an opening-ended paradigm. They were *creating* the economic system inclusive of consumer credit-debt as "inverse-collateral". Credit card thru swipe and the goods go with the purchaser. Implicit, and insidiously here, an economic system was established wherein the economic activities of "the former" were replaced by "the latter": buying by owing to . . . thus not only "inverse-collateral" involved, but a continuity-cost. Purchases far beyond cash-for (at any point of the half-century) were taken home with but the swipe of the card. "The latter", using as their equivalent of consensus-sense what their ascended positions and algorithms and projections otherwise provided them truly superseded "the former". Even to the extent that in many cases you can't use cash. Have to charge it on card.

"The latter", the people of economics controlled "The former", the plain people.

"The former", facing such a revolution of system, and revel-ation in immediate gratification (pay for it little-by-little later, they hoped . . . .), naturally availed themselves of fulfillments and even indulgence. That's human nature. Which, itself, supersedes that mythic mentality -- common sense. For neo-common sense was overwhelmingly, constantly, brainwashingly pummeling the people to perform what the pinnacles of prominence (the GDP Cartel) were promulgating. Common sense now was to take advantage of what the experts advise and provide.

"The latter" (experts) through their dimension of a mythic "common sense in securitizations" (and debt-swaps and derivatives and all) had established what seemed to be a roaring economy. People were financially enabled, thus spending/buying, thus manufacture and travel and other life-amenities were making money, making jobs available. That debt was collateral for such significant levels of economic activity was a synergy!! Interest!!! On time-span payments. And, worst come to worst (for the debtor), maybe best come to best for the return to the lender. Maxed-up level of interest rate ever onward until either final payout/seizure . . . . or default (in which case the write-off to the lender represented a sort of inverse inverse-collateral. The unpaid debt addend became a subtractant from balance sheet and probably a tax advantage. And when "the latter" came to the point of not even holding the debt instruments???? Here was the elixir! The philosopher's stone. Bundle debt and sell it!!!! Sell segments of it, selected and spliced according to some kind of bond or share or buyer thereof. And just in case, take out insurance so that actual loss would be hedged and might (given the slight-probability-of-cataclysm vs. low premium costs) even yield profit! From loss!!

"The latter" (big business and banks and such) created such a hybrid of high finance and high jinx, based on hierarchies: experts, extrapolations of data, algorithms, cyber-computing/conflating/interfacing data for buy-sell instantaneity -- the *profit* production an addend to the "*income*" pool from people-transactions' payments.

"The former" (the populace) . . . anyone would expect their level of calculating abilities (yes, double entendre), let alone math to deal with their end of this brave new world? Hardly. The experts couldn't even grasp it all.

Especially regarding mortgages.

I've read quite a number of times in the last month or so -- that the complexity of mortgage math was even beyond those in the business. No longer did a bank loan money, buyer owe to bank, and a 30-year constancy created carry on. Just from consideration of mortgage multiplicity (variable rates, negative inceptions, pre-pay terms, etc. etc.) it was no longer a bank's having a simple ledger on its mortgagee. When the banks came to sell up/down the line, their "common sense" of what "should" and "ought to" be their criteria for a borrower's eligibility . . . . became somewhat, so soon, a non-issue. As for the big-bank institutions that up-sucked the illusory fertilization of these little squiggles of valuation, so complex had globalization become, that only

few even of those up in the Elysian Fields of finance saw that the impressive swell of portfolios was . . . .an overheated Ponzi-pregnancy of the whole economic system. Not a breeding bonanaza.

And of the few who sensed . . . . it was mostly their intuition as evidentiary element. Not even they had ACTUAL PROOF (documentation). . . . . even of Madoff.

For what can be derived from derivatives but a squaring of the eventual approach to zero??
. . . . one . . . *singularity* sensation . . . . . .da-data-data. . da. . . daaa . . .

So, simply, the highest levels of expertise didn't do their "should " or "ought to". So why assume the rank and file of risk and finance would have the means to measure all the ramifications and rampantifications of the economy? Of course they couldn't.

But more to a point, if not the point. They didn't. Neither "The former" nor "The latter" acted wisely. In part, this was because "wisdom" is an "Heisenbergian construct". There's the ongoing *"uncertainty"* of whether one point's wisdom will be such at another point of economo-socio-space/time. Also, one's wisdom is so often not another's even unto the differential perspective seeming "idiocy".

And here we get back again to a term I used right at the beginning of this diatribe.

"Free-market individualism".

Whether of "The former" or "The latter", an absolutely free market process may become a paradigm of pure possessiveness (MY WAY OR NO WAY). For one's free marketeering maneuvers and even malfeasances represent to him his dog-eat-dog Darwinian superiority if not supremacy. An absolutely free market is not absolutely free for its mass of members. At least it becomes not (and started out as not -- from Genghis *et al* all through Feudalism and former Baronial times even in the U. S.). Established systems from conquering hordes to cornered markets enslave, enserf, or ensnare, not free the general populace.

And, further, that which is (has become) a controlling Carnegie, cartel, corporation, or other private-enterprise "entity" is actually the **governing** system of its concern (mining, manufacture, railroads, even derivatives) and far beyond (raw resources through processing vs. competition plus profit).

Thus the private enterprise is the government if we remove government itself!!!!

Removing government itself takes from the market and social and economic and ecologic equation of action and interaction almost everything other than the closed-circuit quest of the private enterprise -- bottom-line. Well, top line, too, has become pretty much a priority: how many millions the CEO gets or walks away with even when dismissed.

People comprise the actual government.

People is the "management" (and above) of private enterprise.

People of government represent an input ratio (or dimension) deriving from diverse levels, interests, demographics, etc. . . . as well as those who act as liaisons for the interests, principals, principles (and lack thereof) of the private sector.

People of private sector (primarily "corporate") governance are hugely less diverse in their concerns, which are overwhelmingly to make profits, to profit from the making in their own upper-level incomes and options.

People of government, though including a spectrum from diverse demographics and economics, aren't representative of any rabble or eco-nut or socialism-seeking subversion of free enterprise/Capitalism. A significant number of those in Congress have been and are quite wealthy: and for many years now, what with oversight and controls, they didn't get rich from "brown-bagging", from K-Street-direct-deposits, and certainly not from their salaries. Most of those who are rich came from riches. Others (Clinton, an admirable example of achievement on merit or at least intelligence/charisma/etc -- forget personal ethics, of course) . . .others made government their private enterprise thru perseverance and prominence (but that required the backing and fund-fronting of others).

From the Founding Fathers through the Roosevelts and Kennedys and Bushes and maybe inclusive of Mitt, the very leaders of the country have significantly been backed by "dynasty". Presidents, especially of late, have run on the financing of major private enterprises and people (greater than grass-roots pittances). From Soros to Adelson, the mega-contributions. From Exxon, HP, Tyson, Cargill, Caterpillar, ... the major private industry input . . . . thus investment in . . . . thus obligation *by* government's people to promote the purposes of those who provided the "venture capital" of these upstarts' political startups and ongoing political careers!

But at least the people of the government include many who take into even priority account the value that environment, education, medicine, foods, sanitation, and such represent as the whole population's survival; but actual national detriment, too, if allowed to deteriorate or diminish.

The people of private industries have traditionally not shared such survey, nor much given a shit how much shit their processes have produced, piled, percolated, or even poisoned!!

The diverse-dimension of government's personnel protects people per se. Thus there have been rules established for workplace safety, wage levels, benefits, etc. To recognize that "labor" is actually the "capital of Capitalism" (without it who would make or do what makes the money secondarily? . . . But job security added to things enumerated just above) just doesn't appear clearly in the *fundamentalist* perspective of free-market milieu.

From Forbes, August 20, 2012. Excerpts: (here, a case of *extremist* . . .)

> *"Americanism means individualism, but 'Hire American' is collectivist, urging businesses to pay more just to patronize 'our guys'. This is not rational patriotism, it is not Americanism, it is primitive tribalism.*
>
> *Purchasing labor services abroad, if it saves money, is beneficial to everyone, including American workers. Outsourcing does not destroy American jobs, it simply changes the kind of work Americans specialize in. If fewer Americans need to work in manufacturing, then more Americans will be hired in nonmanufacturing jobs. That's The Law of Comparative Advantage, covered in any decent economics text . . . . ."*

" . . .A Congressional Medal of Honor should go to the CEO who cuts his costs the most, whether he does it by outsourcing or any other means."

"Outsourcing Is The U.S. At Its Best"

Harry Binswanger - Capital Flows

Maybe, were there other jobs . . . . but unless the unemployment level since the start of the "Great Recession" of late is a lie, . . . there aren't!! Here.

And even there? The offshores to which almost our whole national heavy industry and manufacturing sailed during the last decades? Unless there's an economic "surge" so that spending can resume here (spending = buying), will there be a decrease in the selling there and thus of the need to manufacture over there?? And if there is an economic "surge" here, will it be Trojan horse precursor for emergent insurgent inflation? Or/also just another bubble of irrational exuberance . . . to burst/bust?? Here and there and everywhere global?

Free market individualism by "The former" or "The latter" needs an operant level, leeway, yes, but with controls. By others than the "marketeers" themselves.

For despite what "should" be or "ought to" be, obviously things didn't work out that way and wouldn't again if unfettered free-for-all market manias ensue again.

Private party "free market individualism" is but naiveté significantly due to the complexity of our economy and its divisions, devices, divisiveness, deviances, diversions, derivatives. It was (at least) not ignorance or irresponsibility alone to account for some-one's taking out a high-point or variable-jump mortgage when the ongoing-seemingly-to infinity of real estate values meant that by getting into the property at point A, it could be re-financed at point B and yield cash appreciation for whatever . . . . or just flipped.

Free market individualism, operated from its position of "wisdom" (taking advantage of opportunity's "operant-spectrum", by which I mean a projected period of time in which further moves would prove profitable to the individual) . . . . free market individualism took out the usurious rate "sub-prime" loans, primarily for rewrites!!! Not initial property purchases. Not alone from the mortgage/loan company's spiel was there influence. There was the evident. Bi-part. Who cares if you're paying extra 6% when your property's going to soar up 18%, given the proof of trend. And what the actual investors were doing.

On the one hand, many were pulling out equity, even debt-equity, to play the housing market. On the other hand, some who re-mortgaged were doing so to initially lower payments and thus hang onto their troubled property at least until things would improve for them. And on a third hand, a whole retired demographic was picking up and moving to better climes such as Florida's and assuming that even if their health shit hit the fan, at least they'd always be able to sell their homesite for at least what they'd paid.

From my reading, semi-extensive, it seems that mortgages given at the behest of Fannie or Freddie and creating "nightmares on Elm -- and every other -- St.) in order to give destitute

minorities their own piece of earth (not quite "Jeffersonian" pie)* . . .seems that wasn't the case.
*as in "The Jeffersons"

Countrywide and others semi-autonomous from Fed Reg, often in collusion with StateReg because of bank pressures, their vast volume of subprime, and actually "toxic" mortgages were the re-mortgaging for and of a diverse demographic. Think how many McMansion-scale defaults, such as in Vegas, or Condos in Miami!! Gated communities with squatters now infiltrating and now peeing in the algae-clogged swimming pools. Not to many American-dream aspirant *indigents* were those loans rigged/written!! The housing collapse (which took along with it much else) didn't result from do-gooder "a home and an acre" (in "Reconstruction the promise was a mule and and 40 acres . .) out-pouring of socialistic idealism or blatant voter-baiting. It was economy's systemic failure.

Had the plain people of free market individualism projected all the possibilities, probabilities, paranoid protectionism of their selves would have usurped the rather incredible economic growth from post WWII up until just those few years ago. There would have been a "preemptive recession", so to speak.

At least to me, from my perspective, "should" and "ought to" have included such dire possibilities as losing a job, house value decrease, and other incentives for me to invest in playing it safe by not playing at all!! My economic advisors consider my stance with almost bemused annoyance. Were I not so "conservative", they'd make a lot more off me. And I might make a lot more off me. But I don't take chances of losing a whole lot (even if not all) to possibly make even quite a bit more (than I actually did: Enron, Lucent, etc.)

But heaven forbid the rest of the people were all as careful and frugal as I.

But, heaven help us, for it was the aspiration to affluence and the acting thereon that:

Brought about the great growth of the economy of the last decades
even inclusive of the off shoring labor and attrition-to-big-box
of *really* private prior enterprises so much

Brought the whole astoundingly complex complex down, analogous to how
an "immune complex" can devastate an organism. An "immune complex"
forms by the integral binding of an antibody to an antigen, and when deposited
in an organ results in disease (such as lupus, erythematosis, rheumatoid
arthritis, scleroderma, and others).

Do we all see how "bundling" into derivatives resembles the just-above?
In investment organs of the economic "body"???

Frankenstein monsters, monetary . . .?

Ultimate expertise failed to foresee, forestall.

Greenspan himself advocated letting market forces do the corrective determinations.
The hierarchy of institutions were divided between absolute scoundrels of originators, and

the bastions of international banking who bought the bundles, having bought into the extrapolations and projections of their high-level experts, algorithms, transaction-instantaneity (to "correct" for "blips") . . . . and AIG on call if fail else all.

Another, almost obverse, perspective of "free market individualism".

Regarding "The former." (the populace).

The people, the overall distribution and demographic of the supposed 90% hold the assumed 2% wealth of the nation (somewhere around there, considering that, like one point something percent of the population is held to control some 90 plus % of the wealth.)Yes, include in the 90% "people" those who get welfare, food stamps, WIC, and other perhaps more entitled entitlements (such as for legitimate disabilities and for unemployment, etc.)

Whatever "The former" (the general population) brings in . . . goes right back out. To the mortgage or landlord, to the grocer or pharmacy, the car payment or rapid transit, the cable and phone bills, to booze stores, to clothing and furnishing and even frivolity now and then here and there (amusement park or something) . . . . everything that they derive "from the system" (be it from wages or "dole") goes right back in.

EVERYTHING. Who, on the population-breadth level, has anything leftover?

So even the "entitlements", after an in-one-hand-and-out-the-other of the recipient, ultimately/rapidly revert into the economy. And into the tax base into which those pay --those to whom the recipient has paid for whatever substance or service.

Recirculation. Pour-up even from trickle-down?

Free market individualism of "The former" (the population) does not amass wealth, thus extract it from the economy. (Only at an economic level of homeowner is there a form of wealth-accretion. This is equity, which is not amassing or extracting from the economy. Obviously it's just a "deferred payment paradigm". And, less so obvious, property appreciation is not an economic substantive until acted upon, "cashed-in" etc. As we've seen, even almost exponential appreciation is but a construct!! A conspiracy?)

To look at economy as a system of circulation, its procedures and processes can be recognized as scientific, technological. If a vast vessel (population group) obtaining disbursement from the economy . . . . returns it all back into the economy via cost of living etc. . . . . . what's happening to the "reservoir" being emptied?

To look and see that this vast sub-system just recirculates what flows into it, one should be led to look elsewhere for what's become the demonstrable dessication.

Free market individualism of "The latter" (the economics echelon) is a fair focus for finding out where the fault may lie. It seems not so much a leak is the problem. No, it's more like **1)** an evaporation.

The recent "debt-standard" (securitized whatevers) was a collateral basis

for purchasing, accreting, incurring. From the credit card to the home equity loan to the tranch-tailored derivatives, to the influence-inflated credit raters' ratings . . . . . the overheat of exuberance (actually, mania) created "steam-liquidity". And it evaporated!

But it also significantly **2)** involves a "big-suck scenario".

In the "distribution of wealth" in this country (hell, in the world, actually), it's obvious that the major "entitlement" is taken out of the overall economy to provide for multi-million dollar incomes for that elite few. Only a portion of that goes back into . . the economy . . . for a substantial amount is retained up in the high-end, highly restricted "eddy" of elitist economic circulation.

Any argument that "they" have "earned" their "free market individualism" demands for limitless riches poses disproportion as deserved dispensation. The Darwinian (actually somewhat an inapt term) success of someone should not equate with a supremacy that extracts excess even just within the closed-context of the guy himself. Someone who can earn $5 million a year just might be able to find enjoyment by getting by on keeping just $2 million after paying into some context of value and responsibility and "should" and "ought" rather than almost autistic self-centricity!!

When what we've assumed as America's success as a nation, society, people, is being closed (parks, police and fire stations, highway rest areas) -- terminated (school athletic and arts programs, elder care transportation and facilities) -- laid off (public works employees including teachers, varied private enterprise personnel in down-sizings) -- and more . . . .)

What's happened to what was providing for these aspects of our American values, ethics, our American. . .way . . of. . . life . . .?

The majority of immigrants have come, legally or illegally, into this country to work. And the majority do. The "Hispanic" varietal-influx? Check out hotels and freight docks and anything else blue collar . . and more and more are upward mobile with training and education. Within a couple generations from now the Hispanic should be no more looked on as some alien (or sedition) element than came to be the Italians and Irish (who were horrendously even hated back in the late 1800s and into early 1900s).

Not the "lower classes". Not the broad population demographic. Not the immigrants. to blame. Until eight or nine years ago there was no "problem unemployment" level. Not the other minorities. It's only the minor minority of any of these who really suck off the system, sequentially sometimes, generation after generation. Once considered human "constitutional" defects (or "bad blood") by the Eugenics Movement -- this demographic fraction is the result of what I call "*Transgenetic* inheritance of their environment", now actually a scientific area termed "epigenetics". Again, though, even the free-loaders unload whatever dole they get right back up into the totalic economic flow.

Yes, some "should". Some "ought to".

Especially "The latter" atop the ladder. Ought to be responsible to more.

Yes, so many are. And were it not for those at the top (who don't shut-off their concept of "success" at a "glass bottom" below which they'd not deign to disperse their largesse) . . . were it not for many of the @379 billionaires in this country (recent Forbes -- and god knows how many probably thousands of millionaires) . . . there wouldn't be culture, charity, hospital wings, art stipends, the opera, much of PBS funding (although the majority thereof now seems to require that the "P" stand for "Private", especially "P" as in Prominent corporations paying the way).

And any idea of actual <u>wealth</u> distribution would be even more suicidal than the recent attempts at amassing "wealth through transmutations". The reservoirs, cisterns, tanks, and even varied vessels of "capital" are indispensable for the hydraulic system of our economy to function fully. And dividing up the wealth totally would provide everyone with hardly a good day's pay . . . . and just be an interim within the process that would result in, again, wealth <u>dys</u>tribution. And the means for that end are absolute requisites for our system (Capitalism) and for those most successful (Capitalists).

But the cyclic *cumulative* end-result, as at present, results in hardships for so many, yet excessive affluence for so few,

The profits of American corporations, as at present, result in losses of jobs which would pay the willing. And even into which some of the lesser willing would be mandated to work to earn their keep. But offshore labor is just soooo cheaper . . . thus our bottom line so higher and managers' millions so morer.

And "free market individualism" is, after all, the infrastructure of the free market economy. The person is the individual. His performance his primacy, his prestige, his portfolio, and even port for his yacht.

But what about his country? His countrymen?

In both "The former" (us-es) but especially "The latter" (the thems) shouldn't there be a priority beyond personal? Beyond primacy?

Should there not, too, be "**free market identificationalism**" -- that one identifies with others? Empathy. Caring. Sharing. Making sure the system works for all?

For what are the alternatives?

Drastically cut social security? With an imminent immensifying old age population?

Go back to pre-Obama and let millions have no health insurance?

Cut off welfare programs and let them beg in the streets or starve

Let there be homeless, who cares from the co-ops and Conn.claves?

(There have been alternatives…seen most often in French history . . . and Russian . . .)

Should". "Ought to".

Almost beside the points above.

The point to those points will be what will result if our lack of caring is the stimulus for what effect it will be the cause!!!

It's a matter of, yes, cause and effect. Not right or wrong. Not should or ought.

And those crowds who could become the madding, the maddened, must, themselves, be recognized as a potential portrayal of <u>their</u> perspective of . . . . thus their valid enactment of their free market individualism . . . .

An email from one of my correspondents concludes with his fear that multinationalism and –culturalism In this country will bring us only "friction and entropy". My response was that, on the contrary at least after an interim, the result will be synergy and creativity, social and commercial.

But during that interim (really up until the early 20th century or so), . . . well, the first of the following pages should sufficiently convey where things were at.

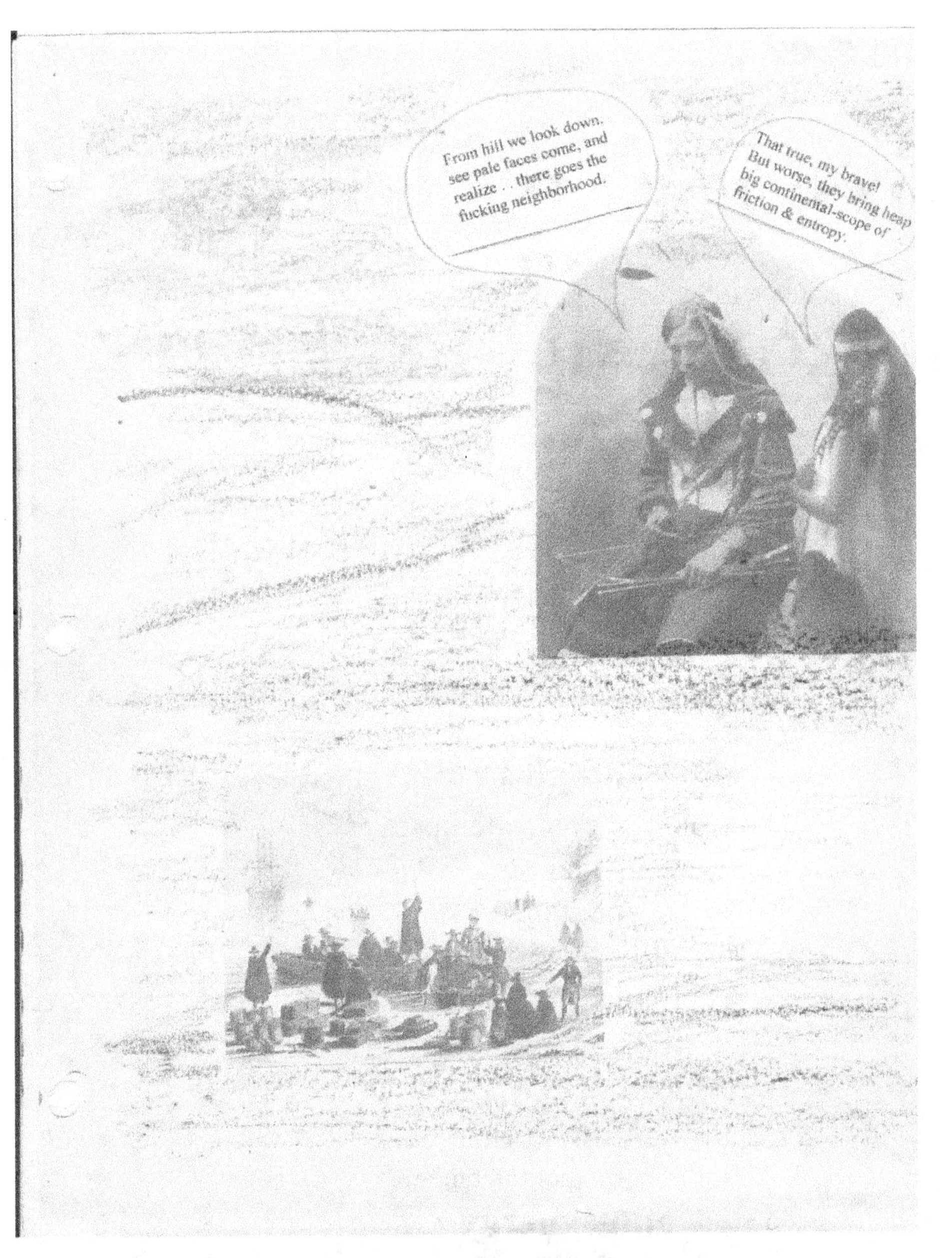
From hill we look down, see pale faces come, and realize . . there goes the fucking neighborhood.
That true, my brave! But worse, they bring heap big continental-scope of friction & entropy.

FISSION AND ENTROPY
OR
SYNERGY AND CREATIVITY

CONTENTS

THE LEGEND (It's satire. **Satire**!!)

Oh yes, as we look back we surely can see
There was chaos and carnage, outright cruelty.
There was genocide, slavery, and prejudice
Exploitation, oppression, crime and caprice.
Though pervasive of all, both invader and -ee,
Through a century, at least, if not more's history
"Entropy" 's meaning would actually betray us
Analysis showing 'twas more like pure chaos!!

From beginning 'twas ordained that Redskins bite dust.
For the history we'll write'll show that we b'longed here fust.
Yes, in Manifest Destiny do we all trust.
(Oh sweet land of liberty, liberated of the squatters)

Williams, demanding church and state separate
And religion as freedom – almost suffered bad fate.
But Roger, dodger, escaped Puritan Inquisition to R. I. state.

About next were the Catholics who had to move out
for the Puritan fathers were very devout
and such heathen invaders could not stay about.
(Oh Maryland, my Maryland . . .)
Yes, England, the motherland, nursed our young land.
She lent us her strength and her money, her hand.
Well we showed that old bitch mother-fuckin' is grand.
(satire, satire)
(Oh Yankee diddle went to town)
A machine to build railroads brought in 'cross the seas
an' you don't have to feed it or care it it freeze
an' it's slimy and yellow and called the Chinese
(Oh I be workee onee rairoa)
Soon them stinkin' redskins they all bit the dust
and we'll write in the history books we was here fust
'cause in Manifest Destiny do we all trust
(sweet land of liberty / liberation from aboriginal populace)

The farmers built fences, their harvest to reap,
but the cattlemen shot them and hatred ran deep
'cept when some lonely farmer needed a good night's sheep)
(. . . I want ewe, I want ewe so baa-aa-a-ad . . .)
Then claim jumps and land grabs and scandals and all
and railroad safaris made buffalo fall
and we'll all swing our partners at the extinction ball
(Oh give me a home where the.buffalo [and all else] roamed)
You're reading satire!! Please don't be like
a few others who've read this and threatened
me with bodily harm.
The South vs. North, such a great thing to see
all the carnage a suffering so the slaves could be free
to make room for the North's new farm *machinery.*
(. . .as we go burning through Georgia . . .)
We stood up for peace, for justice and law
an' we protected the weak from the strong, and you saw
how we protected poor, helpless li'l Texas in the Mexican War.
(Oh give me land, lots of land . . .)
Well son of a bitch, it's the tired and the poor
from some teeming shores to America's lure. *(it's satire!!)*
All Irish will kindly report to the sewer.
("Why'd I ivver come across the sea from Ireland?)
Sheeit, them Niggers, of course, they're always around.
Where there's no opportunity or pay they're still found.
No wonder them coons never gits off the ground.
(Them boonas, them boonas gonna walk aroun' . . .)
But the Krauts and the Polacks, Chinks, Gooks Catholics
and the Boogies, Kikes, Wops, the Ruskies and Micks,
hand-in-hand became brothers . . ..to dump on the Spics.
(Make of our hearts one heart . . . .)

Yes, we came a long way in this land of the free:
There was M. Luther King, there was John Kennedy.
There was John's brother Robert, just mentioning three.

And there is so much else that makes everything great.
Like the FBI, CIA, KKK, IRS an' still racial hate.
And what the military-industrial complex and petrochemical cartels and bio-pharmaceutical corporations and cloning and carrion-fed cattle and fast foods soon may create . . . . . .

(*SATIRE*! You've read satire.
Don't be upset with me.)

You write in your email . . . .

"We know that the latter [big gov't] are [sic] primarily responsible for big projects, those that citizens and small biz can't carry out on their own."

There are some *big* projects that big business can't carry out on their own, unless conducted by consortium or other corporate collaboration ("joint ventures"). Mobilization and warfare is the extreme "endeavor", things such as the Interstate System, NASA, and many more are also beyond just big business basis. In these cases, the government is actually . . in business with the businesses.

In such cases, "big gov't" actually plays a co-corporate role, providing funding, from R&D to implementation and exploration -- space, yes, but also with regard to the biggest of the big businesses (such as Petro, Pharma, Agri), ... tax, subsidy, rights, Army Corp collaboration, and such.

"From two sources: does it work efficiently . . . " you ask.

"Efficiency" here needs specification, definition, case-determination. Prior to government (as societal, environmental, and other checks and balances on private enterprise autonomy) . . . back when "government" was hardly more than the brown-bag-recipient-crowd to "legislate the legitimacy-documentation" of whatever the corporate, trust, and cartel collusions and connivances wanted . . . .

Back then the "efficiency" of private enterprise:

Devastated large spans of land with water-pressure "mining", the run-off silting streams and rivers and even into estuaries and San Fran Bay, resulting in massive Salmon (and other specie) regional extinctions.

The conditions of miners (and their minors), still often horrendously evasive of safety, were essentially oblivious to personnel as other than replaceable parts in the mining machinery. It took the emergent -- government-as-representative-of-populace -- and premise (environment) -- to at least try to alleviate the squalor, malnutrition, black lung, and frequent explosive or collapsive deaths.

In the Carnegie (and other) steel mills, conditions were bad, though not frequently fatal. Twelve-hour shifts, six days a week. Rotating shifts, and the shift coming off nights would put in 24 hours straight for the first day of day and vice versa.

Two holidays per years were provided, neither paid (Xmas and Thanksgiving). No comp. No unemployment insurance.

No wage guarantee and when Carnegie's profits lagged, he cut his workers' hourly pittance-wages of survival!!
(read *Sparrow Point; Making Steel* and others)

When, especially in NewYork City (though I assume elsewhere), fire companies were essentially private enterprises (quasi-militias?), one company would battle another for the right (and the income/confiscation) for putting down the fire and taking off with the salvageables . . . while the building would burn, sometimes to the ground. Before government got involved, what "hydrants" there were would sometimes be concealed by one brigade so that another wouldn't know their location!!

Before, well, not long ago down South there was a representatively reprehensible case of private enterprise protecting its interests without the over-reaching interference of government. It was some chicken-processing plant with its exits locked to prevent worker sneak-outs. Alas, the fire. This was in violation of what govt. (as representative of its electorate, at least in part) had at least accomplished by enacting regulations.

The Triangle Shirtwaist Company Fire of 1911 (Gina DeAngelis), relates the pre-regulatory situation so common & in this case, so tragic. Women. Paid by the piece. Four hundred girls. Others working in other factories in the building -- total some 2000. Only two elevators. 12 floors. Triangle Co on 5th. " 'The shop is swept only once a week; the air is so close that sometimes you can hardly breathe . . . . in the busy season . .. I put in what equals eight work-days in the week. Thirty minutes is allowed for lunch, which I must eat in the dressing room four flights. above the shop, on the ninth floor" . . . . "the boss paid me three dollars a week.'." quoted from a worker's quote in the book "Aside from horribly unsanitary working conditions, many workers suffered from the whims of their bosses, who were not above 'dirty tricks' to get more work out of them." "Average income about $250 a year."

"A study of 1,243 shops in New York City . . . a few months before the Triangle fire, had yielded . . . .appalling findings. The board's report, which was published in a magazine only nine days before the Triangle fire, noted the following hazardous conditions:

"Ninety nine percent of the shops were found to be defective in respect to safety; 14 had no fire escapes; 101 had defective drop ladders; 491 had only one exit; 23 had locked doors during the day; 58 had dark hallways ; 78 had obstructed approaches to fire escapes; and 1,172 or 94 percent had doors opening in instead of out. Only one [shop] had a fire drill."

The site of the Triangle fire, The Asch Building, had a fire escape (unusual for the time), but that ended over a skylight and, with other buildings since erected, a courtyard, thus requiring escapees to access the street by going through the building!!

"Because of the shortage of inspectors, factory owners and bosses could predict -- or pay bribes to be warned -- when inspectors were due to arrive."

In the Triangle tragedy, piled-up trimmings and silt caught fire . Exits to stairs were blocked both by debris and by fire. 146 workers perished, some jumping from the windows, others burning in situ.

This and myriad other labor/safety/exploitation/jeopardy situations in which the government eventually became involved (up to and including OSHA) hardly represent any over-reaching, interference, or socialistic-usurpation of the private sector's self-determination except in criminal neglect against humanity.

Before the eventual EPA, timber clear-cutting and prairie sod-busting resulted in drastic environmental degradation including the dust-bowl conditions and exodus of so many of its residents from that soup of silt.

But back to New York prior to government . . over-reaching? (I've touched on some of this before). Early land holding: Rensselaerswyck Manor 830,000 acres

"Lower Manor"	250,000
Livingston	160,000
Castleton	25,000 on Staten I.
Macomb	1,000,000 grab from Iroquois

Astor, by 1830 was richest man in U.S., from furs, tea, opium -- combined wealth into NY R. E. purchase.

But onward here, review of pre-government intervention until the late 19th c.

One way to avoid the taint of blackness was to loudly assert whiteness, and the Irish quickly learned that in New York City blacks could be despised with impunity. Another route to permanent certification as members of an Anglo-Celtic racial majority was through affiliation with Tammany Hall. Northern Democrats had bonded with southern planters in a common negrophobia; now racism would do similar duty on the home front, smoothing divisions between New York's Angles and Celts, allowing the party to swell its ranks from both sides. The theater, too, allowed white working people of all backgrounds to come together as an audience to laugh at derogatory representations of black "others." Not surprisingly, minstrel songs singled out abolitionists—particularly Arthur Tappan—for merciless ridicule. Indeed abolitionism and blackface ascended the political stage arm in arm.

"HE CALLED MY SAVIOUR A NIGGER!"

In May and June of 1834, Arthur and Lewis Tappan stepped up their abolitionist drive. Among other initiatives, they underwrote formation of a Female Anti-Slavery Society. The participation of white ladies in a mixed-race movement jangled the nerves of New York racists—which were soon further tautened by pronouncements from the Rev. Samuel Cox, the antislavery (and anti-Catholic) cleric.

Arthur Tappan was a pewholder in Cox's Laight Street Church. One Sunday morning on his way to church, Tappan encountered Samuel Cornish on the street. As Cox's institution was nearby—two miles closer to Cornish's home than where the black clergyman usually worshiped—Tappan invited him in, and the two sat together in Tappan's pew. This led to a tremendous row, with some church members threatening to resign and the elders insisting that Tappan not repeat the offense. (Arthur would never again be seen in public with any of his African-American associates, even one as light-skinned as Cornish.) Cox, however, chided his congregation for its intolerance. Arguing that as Christ was probably of a dark Syrian hue, he might well have been ejected along with Cornish, Cox denounced "nigger pews" and called for church integration. He was instantly subjected to citywide attack. As one merchant spluttered, "And would you believe it? he called my Saviour a nigger! God damn him!"

By June lurid rumors were flying around town (recycled by colonizationalist champion James Watson Webb in his *Courier and Enquirer*). The abolitionists—so the stories went—had told their daughters to marry blacks. Arthur Tappan had divorced his wife and married a Negress. Presbyterian minister Henry Ludlow was conducting interracial marriages. Abolitionists were encouraging black dandies to parade up and down Broadway on horseback to seek white wives. William Leete Stone, secretary of the New York Colonization Society and editor of the *Commercial Advertiser*, joined in stoking popular fury, assuring his readers that amalgamation appealed only to those of "morbid or vicious tastes." A startled English traveler reported that even the "nicest people" talked about "sexual passion, with a vehemence of manner, and in a tone of earnestness, utterly abhorrent from the generally received notions of propriety."

There were some 60,000 horses in NY City. They produced some 60,000 gallons of urine and 2.5 million pounds of manure per day. . . piling up and oozing out from the streets.

The wedding of Jay Gould's daughter cost $5.5 million

The age of consent, which had been 10, was raised to 16 in 1889. Brothels were omnipresent.

In 1895, 6,000 sweatshops. Girls worked 15 to 18 hours a day, often no talking and bathroom "privileges" severely controlled

Vanderbilt's daughter married to 9th duke of Marlborough at the cost of 50,000 shares of Beech Creek Railway and payments for rehabilitation of Blenheim Palace and construction of Sutherland House in London . . to the total of more than $10 million.

T. Roosevelt becomes Commissioner of Police. "What this city needs is a war!!" to relieve the economic disasters, unemployment excess, crime, filth, and all else which beset it during these pre-big-government-intrusion days of the great American dream of equal opportunity (including the pursuit of happiness) for all.)

Completion of the Transcontinental Railroad puts some 20,000 Chinese out of work, thus into the work-seeking force, exacerbating extensive discrimination ("anti-Sinoism"?). Chinese immigration curtailed, and even consideration of expulsion of the race back to China.

Primarily Chicago -- how about the pre-government-regulation era of the meat-packing industry (*The Jungle* by Upton Sinclair).

A personal experience of the pre-regulatory ethos of the trucking industry: I'd made a run from Billerica, Ma to Presque Isle, Maine. Delivered a heavy " floor load" (all had to be lifted box-by-box onto pallets). Without respite I drove back South, passing again through the peak foliage of the Allagash Wilderness which stretched almost infinitely around me but its vivid colors of yellow wafting in the breeze transmuted to Caterpillar earth-moving equipment attacking . . . and the reds were revised into emergency vehicles perhaps coming to my rescue from the yellows. . . and indiscriminate colors of foliage I hallucinated as cows and horses and. . . . how I ever made it back to Mass. without falling asleep in transit I don't remember (maybe I was asleep. . .) At the truck terminal I turned in my papers.

Terminal manager approached me. "Hook to trailer #xxxxx. It's a time-sensitive for Elizabeth (N.J.) and there's nobody else can take it."

"I've just run 30 hours straight with no sleep," I announced.
"The load's got to go."
"I gotta sleep." I walked out the door.
Prior to any government-agency (we didn't have union) protection, he could very well have followed-through on his stated intention to fire me.

And now, still, we have such important, perhaps crucial, concerns. One is the environment. Private enterprise is significantly if not entirely, focused on its bottom-line of product-sales. Government oversight unto regulation was (lead, asbestos, bad meat, bad medicine, etc.) and still is a necessity. It may over-reach, even intrude, in cases. But just in case, better the big brother's breadth of concern than the little brats' priority of just getting their own way$.

The atmosphere is part of the environment. But I'll mention it in this separate paragraph. Was it government over-reach, socialism in clean-air's cloaking, closing the incinerators of the 50s? (After the great waste-to-meat experiment industrial-dimension piggeries as the urban and rural garbage disposal technology of pork manufacture), but prior to the incinerators, was it over-reach quenched the open-burning of dumps? (read *Garbology* & others)

And the lead from the gasoline . . . .

And now the regs regarding emissions, with the fascinating government "dispensation" to Navistar of violation-allowed-for-fines-paid (to prevent the company from having to shut down and put all its and its ancillaries' employees out of work.). And the other engine makers have sued (and so far won their case) to prevent the exemption for Navistar!! Do we here have a case of over-reach of private enterprise, interfering with the benign efforts of government to preserve a major private enterprise and its work-force?? (a case of what I've termed the reciprocity of private enterprise cannibalism)

I think the above suffices as my considerations of your points up to the point of your email where you state . . . " . . . ."gov't attention, (law, mandate, regulation, etc.)? And can we afford the whole thing after years of vote buying and generally living beyond our means?"

Your (just quoted) statement seems like a concatenation of disjoints. Is "vote buying" (which would primarily be a private-sector-sin euphemized as "subsidy" or "pork" -- but also a requisite of economies of our scale) -- is it any factor in an equation of what we can afford? And what does "afford" entail? Mere monetary? Or does it include ecological, sociological, even international considerations of cause-effect in consideration of a breadth of concerns and categories, resources, trade, détente, ...

And . . . "generally living beyond our means" . . . . .

What constitutes "beyond our means"? Who, specifically, is/are "we", thus who comprise the "our"?

Is it "beyond our means" to provide public-sector police- and firemen?

Is it "beyond our means" to keep libraries open, especially since many of them were built and booked by the bequests of Carnegie?

Is it "beyond our means" to have school supplies supplied by the schools supported by the public sector (taxes) or should teachers have to pay for the stuff out of their salaries? Are sports and arts programs expendable "*beyonds*" in "the means" of our economic distributions?

Is it "beyond . . " to provide, though "subsidized", a sanitary and fed and housed survival for the under-class of economic ascent and accomplishment? Or would it be better to let them go hungry and replace the missing horse-shit in the city streets? Should the elderly be no longer coddled in the "beyond", rather they should be forced to take charge of their own affairs by way of investments in dot.coms or derivatives or real estate trusts or all those other so-highly-profitable-and-predictably-exponentiating portfolios of the private sector?? Is Social Security beyond reason?

Beyond reason? Beyond resources? Health care? Including those aspects that protect injured workers, disabled anyones, the elderly indigent, the loonies and retards and that whole ensemble of the incapacitate . . . .

As we look really critically, closely, just what segment/echelon of society has been living beyond [our] means? It surely doesn't seem to be the "lower class", the infirm, the aged, the incapacitated, even the "masses" of populace of which the special needs (or for the slackers even specious needs) are but subset minorities.

If the comprehensive protections and benefits (societal, environmental, and otherwise) we've brought about as "America" are an untenable entitlement ("let them not eat Whoopie-pies", also, **they** don't pay their fair share for the air to be unpolluted . . .), then where are the jobs in which **they** could *earn* their dole? Or if the survival of reciprocity-cannibalism-survival-of-the-fittest laissez-faire capitalism of our corporations can only be achieved by third- and fourth-world wages, maybe our whole system of "economy" is a bankruptcy. Of our country and its un-portfoliated populace. The wealth is securely with the wealthy, it seems.

Consider (as I have in prior pieces). Economy is a circulation. Let's look at the bottom-level. Welfare or food-assistance or whatever . . recipient gets the dole. Every cent goes back into the infrastructure of private-enterprise economy: the grocer, the baker, the landlord, the utilities, the cable and phone bills, some liquor, etc. etc.

That "trickle-up" (or "sucktion") passes through the retail into the wholesale on to/through transportation and unto the manufacturing and even beyond into the resources realm for the stuff out of which the products are made. And along the way, at each stage, "endo-tarrifs" (taxes) decant from the flow into the reservoir (including Federal Reserve, also other governmental utilizations of proportionment-derivation. But along the way, the various private-sector levels draw from the flow their sufficient (generally) income-unto-profit.

The poor don't profit, invest, upgrade, amass, horde, extract from the economic mainstream into the tribute-aries of their dividend (or cashed-in speculation) incomes. Such upper-level economy (wealth) doesn't interface with overall economic flow. Doesn't really even trickle down!! Except through the gov't tapping the recluse resource of the riches and richest. . . . ..
The most blatant case in point: from, what, 12 years ago there were tax breaks proportionately providing for the wealth and the wealthy instated (and in stated purpose) in order to stimulate the economy, create jobs, establish on-shore business growth . . . . . . thus for private enterprise to provide a viable economic system of investment, employment, wage payment, purchase power, and only the necessary extrapolation of taxation. Wha' happen??

Living beyond . . . our . . . means?? The masses? In the Mattapan (or Southie) tenement (now designated "condo") at $1500 a month plus util?
Living beyond . . . . the modest suburban cape or ranch bet-up to the mid-hundred-thousands by banks bundling mortgages as credit-default swaps to the extent that actual ownership of many abandoned houses is impossible to determine due to the internationalization and fractional ownership of shares?

Seems it's not the "lower class" that's living beyond their means. Maybe it's us? Hardly you, I think, even though "Red Gate Lane" doesn't sound demographically degenerate. But I assume that your position within the economic flow is essentially a re-investment, a flow-back of funds, via your cost-of-living expenses going into the general marketplace, your taxes (and even your cost of reasonable and deserved amenities, luxuries, even cruise).

Surely not me living beyond my means -- sleeping in a pickup truck four nights a week after working 12 hour days (at least) -- then migrating to my $21,500 "estate" in the Shirley trailer park for the 3-day weekend. The level of my "capitalization" and its share-increment and dividend-return is modest by Forbes measure, mere low 7-fig. I've re-invested, "recirculated" not into the

consumer marketplace, but into tuition assistance and charities, "preemptive bequests" to heirs, and in financial and insurance instruments providing for me for whatever duration I'll be.

If not the poor, the masses . . . .if not you . . .. if not me . . . .
Just who are living beyond their means, and drawing out of the economy its flow? Diverting from economy's circulation its volume? Thus the draining designated in part by . . "deficit"??

But could it be, not the class, but the number of them?
Could it actually be the masses after all? The massiveness of the masses!! Too many to be provided for? Well, let them be employed, again I say. Bring back some jobs to our shores. Or create earnings-work here under the auspices of the government (even if this smacks of socialism). But if there's not the money to provide the masses the dole, from whence comes the money to provide them the "public-sector" employment opportunities???
So what's the option? Socio-economic-level selection for extermination?
Or do we need to partially base the economy on something other than, and beyond, producer-consumer procedures, profit and GDP (ever-expanding) thus an equivalent of a Madoff mechanism?

So let's say we implement somehow the means whereby all must be productive in one way or another in order to earn, not be entitled to, their survival incomes/wages. They perform infrastructure services in civic and/or social settings (and there'd be a lot of confrontations with unions, wouldn't there? And unions are not governmental agencies). But the masses would be employed. Earn their keep. Keep probably nothing after cost of living including taxes." Healthy economic -- circulation!!

So we can now look at another group. Those who have been and are and would be (still -- in the just-above utopian scenario) living "beyond [our] means". Those who extract (in wages and options and dividends and liquidations and even golden parachutes) exponentially from the economic flow. Those who bring in multi-million dollars a year, who direct $50 million into the purchase of a yacht into which another $200 million goes for refurbishment and lengthening. Those who erect $75 million dollar mansions with 40 car garages for their exotic and antique collections and even our Presidential-aspirant whose le$$er costly residence will have a car elevator. The CEOs who, despite share-collapse, extract several million per an. from, actually, the shareholders (and thus the broader economy).

The **capital** accretion, accumulation, & accomplishment, of the entrepreneurial echelon is wealth reservoir, storage, cistern, securitization.

The billions-worth of the 397 billionaires listed in Forbes (Oct 10,2011) represents a resource: a monetary equivalent, in a way, to mineral! or even to petro "reserves"! But it could be that the *income* deriving from the billion-level capital is disproportionate, unwarranted. And the use of that income may represent "living beyond our/THEIR means" -- for here the "our" applies to the overall economy, the overall populace dependent upon a viable economic distribution and allocation.

I can't be sure. I don't have statistics. But it seems that the flow from such denominational depths into narrow channels of multi-million dollar yachts, jets, mansions, art (and otherwise), antiques . . . . . denigrates economy by retaining wealth in upper-echelon eddies, so to speak. I can't be sure, but it could be that those ultra-rich could still enjoy their luxuries, indulgences, amenities, and all while returning into the economy-at-large-and-small quite a bit more than they do. Maybe they'd have to sacrifice the gold leaf on the stairwell of the refurbished yacht?

That may represent living beyond economy's means, if economy is to be anything other than extreme indulgence and greedy self-serving folios.

I must also observe that there are many MS sufferers who somehow make do without $100,000 dressage horses as therapy regimens!!

For the mainstream, the masses of Americans, there's high unemployment, foreclosure, school program curtailments, civil servant (fire, police, etc.) shrinkage. There's concern for the liquidity of social security. The cost of health care is beyond the means of millions. And parks and highway rest areas and public swimming pools etc. are being closed.

Maybe what we've assumed to be the great achievement of America has been the "living beyond our means" and only now it's come to collapse? Maybe more distribution from the million-dollar and more per year incomes of the "wealthy" would not irrigate the re-fruition of our economy.

But it would be a resource of recirculation of what is now horded by individuals and corporations both!!!

Miscellaneous considerations via notes and quotes

There was a surplus. Then a Bush.

Then the war. Prior to, Robert Samuelson, in Newsweek, 9/23/'02 wrote under heading "A War We Can Afford?" . . . "A good guess is that a war against Iraq might cost about $40 billion. Even at twice that figure, it would still be less than 1 percent of GDP."

Cost of deployment -- estimates vary, but Congressional Budget Office calculates the cost of preparing for war in Iraq could reach $12.5 billion plus a billion for every month that troops are in action. (another source)

The US spends as much on defense as the 20 next top-spending nations combined.

A billion a week the cost of peace.

"Price Tag Soars In War Vs. Terror -- BUSH ASKS FOR $87 BILLION MORE.

Cost of occupation of Iraq -- $3.9 billion per month

to re-construct damage sustained by Iraq systems and infrastructure due to the war -- $120 billion.

"There are more than 60 private firms employing more than 20,000 people, carrying out military function in Iraq." "Halliburton's Kellog, Brown, and Root division, the largest military firm in Iraq, provides troop supplies and equipment maintenance under a Pentagon contract estimated at $13 billion." (*Outsourcing the War*, Singer in Foreign Affairs, 4/'05).

A congressional study into worldwide weapons transfers reported they were at their highest level since 2000. Total agreements on weapon sales were $37 billion in 2004, a 30% increase on 2003. The United States made the most agreements, taking a third of the market.

U.S. investment in Germany increased 48.5% between 1929 and 1940 . . . while decreasing elsewhere in Europe . . . .

Cheney and his chief of staff -- participated in drafting a 2000 report . . .that called for taking over Iraq . . as part of a larger, oil-minded "Pax Americana".

Despite conflict of interest issues, Bush served on Carlyle's Asian Advisory Board and made highly compensated speeches and trips . . .and helped the group procure well-heeled investors. Twelve rich Saudi individuals and families signed up (including BinLaden family)

I think the latter three ppgs. were from the book,
American Dynasty, a history of the Bush and Walker families.

There came this extravaganza of diverting billions from the U.S. infrastructure and socio-structures into Iraq (first in destructions and then rebuilding inclusive of schools and Saddamless new textbooks).

The billions didn't just disappear down some drain into oblivion. The billions were diverted into military (ever more privatized, even transport and KP activities) and massively into private strategic industries, corporations: the makers of municians and materiel for the "machinery" of war's products.

Obviously the billions from the tax-base and thus de facto not into the domestic drawers for allocations . . . .went into the mega-corporate coffers.

It seems to me, given the outcome (the outflow) of our economy, that "living beyond our means" applies to:

Maximizing profits by off-shoring manufacture, thus jobs
Iraq, which diverted economics into corporates' confines.
Investing/banking based on bundling and bloating values
even to the extent of their obverse (thus almost bankrupting
AIG, the major insurer/hedge for the profit from loss)

The incomes of the CEOs and so many others, and that they can indulge exorbitant high-end economics while even basic pools of funding for the populace are drained.

Goodies? Beyond our means? Mere modest housing and feeding for "the people" even inclusive of a luxury indulgence such as a Whoopie pie on occasion?

Government over-reach in retrospect? Not only did regulations resolve and ameliorate horrific conditions and problems, but the remedies so often resulted in enhanced private-sector growth, innovation, employment.

Efficiency? Think energy efficiency resulting in part from legislation (such as to control emissions and other pollution). From belching stacks of coal smoke to now. . . . . from 12 mpg and maybe 100k mile life expectancy of the vehicle to now . . . . . from incandescent wattage/amperage suck to the varieties of the "intermediate-illuminators" which may well end up bringing LED lighting to be the "given" (and able to be powered by on-site solar and/or wind generation). Government mandates were often catalysts for such advances in technology, even catalytic per se.

Vote buying? By whom? Surely not the populace!! "Hey, Senator, I'll pay you if you back legislation to let me buy Whoopie pies with my food stamps".
If mega-private enterprise (such as Exxon-Mobil, Proctor, Raytheon, Carlyle, et. al. pay into to get that "legislated justification" for . . . which puts people to work for wages as well as puts profit into the portfolios, would not a better term be "vote-investing"?

Living beyond our means . . . . .
Again, now in retrospect of the above . . . .
Who . . . .???

Herewith, and heretofore, I think I've provided sufficient reference material to support my standpoints, and probably try a reader's tolerance of detailed documentation. Be thankful that I haven't imposed upon you the vastly greater extent of notes I've taken from the many books I've read, not only on New York City as criterion (though extreme) of conditions in this country.

Another fascinating book was *Immigrant City*, a history of Lawrence, Ma, a major mill-town from the mid-1800s to early 1900s. when it fell victim of "South-shoring" (not off-shoring, but industries moving from the North to the cheap labor American South).. After a couple decades, massive off-shoring to the dirt-cheap labor force of 3rd and 4th world countries closed the mills in the South that had opened at the expense of the closed mills of the North.

Other matters of mention from *Immigrant City:* As in NYC, the blacks were at the bottom of society. The Irish ("white Niggers") were but a nuance above, perhaps even worse off for their work-ethic, thus suffering in mucking tunnels and digging canals (sometimes with smudge-pots fastened around their necks so the smoke and fumes would at least disperse the mosquitoes and gnats enough for them to be able to breathe). Blacks didn't work out (except in slavery) in such abjectly abusive employment.

From mid-l800s, Irish, but also notably Southern European children including Italian, were considered to be "uneducable", thus "constitutionally" inferior. At present, the only remnant of this "eugenic-relegation" seems to apply to Negros, specifically African-Americans (as opposed to Caribbean or other-origin "coloreds". Even from upper middle-class, suburban, professional-parent families, academic performance of Afro-Americans is abysmal. But this hardly represents any genetic blemish. It's self-assertion, a proclamation of identity independent of the white . . . . through a "heritage" of victimology, anti-intellectualism, thus overcoming the need to functionally overcome anything by taking tribal pride in self-subjugation unto self-ridicule (intra-ethnic use of the term "nigger", manner of dress, etc.).

Italians were despised as almost aboriginal primitives (and those of their nationality achieving success enough to purchase in WASP neighborhoods and plant their tomato plants and grape vines in the front yards of the Victorians) were not welcomed within the Protestant paradigm (all the worse the Virgin statue in the bathtub grotto).

I read somewhere that the " . . .wretched refuse from their teeming shores" in Emma Lazarus's lyrics/poem, actually referred to and was rebuke of the Southern European and Eastern (Russian) Jewish influx from (and bringing with them) the poverty and ignorance and dys-sanitation of the shtetls. . . the rebuke by the already long-since arrived Northern European Jewry. One Jew as antiSemite to another.

I could well have expanded my comments, my context, my few copied references herein, into an actual book-length comparison of then . . . .all along . . . through so much of America's formative history, and now.

We've come a long way. From the drastic discrimination against the French Canadians (not only because of Catholicism -- "Evangeline" . . .) we've long been at the

state of not really paying an attention to whether someone is of French or French-Canadian, or just about any other heritage. So, too, the Irish, now essentially so totally integrated into the "Caucasian" populace as to be all but undifferentiable (unless, for example, by Kennedy-esque exceptionality.

There's still antiSemitism, but practically extinct. From the era when "The American Bar Association" was established, in part, to prevent Yiddish from becoming the *lingua franca* of the legal profession, when Jews weren't allowed in some restaurants or hotels etc., we may note that this or that guy is Jewish (especially how many are in the economic-realm of the federal government), but discrimination unto disenfranchisement has ended long ago.

Italian? Yes, we note names ending with vowels and generally just subliminally associate them with nationality. For the most part, Italian, Greek, Irish, you name him or her, and they're a "societal generic". Caucasians. Inclusive, of course, of English, German, Dutch, Scandanavian, and all the rest (who way back would have been at each other's throats almost as if different, competing-for-territory-and-survival species.)

Blacks, Latinos, Muslims, and others are still definitely delineated, sig-nificantly by their appearance, from complexion to attire. But they're integrated in the jobs, consumer-realms, and even neighborhoods in this country. There may be subtle discrimination, disdain for the chador'd or, especially, burqa'd Muslim woman. But there's no persecution. In years past there would have been.

We've come a long way by integrating astounding ethnic and sociological diversity within a socio-economic format for functioning -- earning, spending, acquiring, having, enjoying the implements and perks of Western civilization! We're all in these together.

We've come through periods of horrific traumas and lesser turmoils, from the Civil War through incipient anarchy (Sacco and Vanzetti), Jewish-communist cells, White Supremacy whackos, McCarthy paranoid pathology, etc. etc.

We've come to the point where the division and contestation and friction of a whole continent's populace is significantly concerned with how much the ultra-rich should have to pay back into economy, share with society.

We've reached a level of socio-cohesion where even in the ranted vitriol of opposing political conventions, not only objectively important matters, but emotional and subjective standpoints are proclaimed from podium to rouse roars from the assembled thousands . . . . . yet even with inclusions of humor or satire.

Through history even unto the present *elsewheres*, the differences between our "right" and "left" would result in reciprocal retaliation, assault, bombings. Now, one candidate seeks to discredit and destroy the adversary <u>Verbally</u>. In our country there have been no

poisonings, shootings, stabbings. We've come a long way from the past of our "family" background in the old countries, from our human heritage still operant in many other contemporary countries' conflicts and contests.

We may have high unemployment and a depressed real estate market (with regionally vacated homes. A bubble (like many before) burst, grounding greed & profiteering. But actions were taken, tranche (toxic-mortgage-bundles) hemorrhages were Fed-transfused. And the organism of (it's now global) economy was kept alive. How much greater the unemployment would be had GM and Chrysler succumbed, shut-down? To what catastrophic extent the domino demise of big-banks had others just been left to the "market forces" which actually, as their "marketing strategy" had led them (and almost to a global extent) to self-destruction!!! AIG, the life-boat for the drowning domains of derivatives, would itself have been dunked. But that didn't happen. We've come a long way up in preventing how far the devastating drop could have been given other times' defaults . . . . . actual faults?

The drastic devastation of actual depression was prevented this time. We've come a long way. There may be high unemployment, but there aren't breadlines, nor hordes riding rail lines. There may be huge deficit, but it's not of the human in actual anguish.

And there is not, realistically, any chance of mass-mobilization for a WW III to restart the economy, re-employ those @8% in jobs or uniforms. Too much the world is an interdependency of mutually maintained infrastructure and hyper structure, import-export, multi-national Corporations' "governance" of commodities, currencies, consumers, complexities otherwise. We've come a long way in this world.

Through the 30 or so books I've read rather specifically concerning the area, I've concluded that synergy, not friction, has been the <u>outcome</u> of America's cultural diversity. From back at the beginning when white invaders of the Indians' neighborhoods were the immigrants, to now . . . ?

Just look at the diversity of nationalities attending major colleges. Just look into, now, the extent of Hispanic entrepreneurship, economic benefit to neighborhood, community, city, state, tax base. There may be clusters of jobless Mexicans standing at the foot of Home Depot lots, hoping for a day's pay with some emerging contractor. But the majority of whatever Latinos are employed. And regarding the argument that they've taken jobs we Anglos should have -- who do you know wants to work hotel housekeeping, foodservice or make migrant agricultural effort your profession?

And though there's despicably widespread poverty, alcoholism, and other afflictions of native Americans "interned" on their res-es, there are those that are significantly profiting from resources, natural and odds-determined!!

For the most part, we've all come together as a synergy-society.

Our present "recession" is but a "blip". It's a cyber-age (derivative-driven) bubble where one's house's ever-incremental value had no basis other than what it could bring if you bailed out before the "correction" when the bubble burst.

The mud-slinging and vitriol-vectoring of recent politics is the obverse of entropy. It's the manifestation of a dynamic *fission* of ideas and ideals and ideologies. As with the *particulate* dimension, only the few facets of the political domain may actually function through polity to fuse into policy. But the dynamism of our system works -- and without mayhem and massacre (other than verbal -- and even that, as noted, with the touches of humor and satire and sarcasm).

Friction? Yes. As frisson. Ongoing. Sequential. Look at the influence of the various nationalities on "American" culture, arts and entertainment. Afro-American music fused classically by Gershwin. Rap now the woofer-assault assimilation of the hi-end WASP young adults. The unwanted Irish for so long so admirably ensconced in politics and all other levels and labors of life. The filthy Italians in, you-name-it-walks-of life as well as in construction. Jews from teeming shores or otherwise have excelled in almost everything, from the highest levels of science to the nadirs of some stand-up entertainment's venues. The vast Hispanic influx provides a truly, admirably, dedicated populace doing the housekeeping, cooking, warehousing, crop-picking, but also ever-emerging into the mainstream of diverse ascent -- in education, income, residence, reciprocating roles in society.

And it's all been working with hardly anyone attacking anyone now years!

And it's all of us working together in combination as a culture of multi-culturalism.

And in all the above -- my point of contrast to yours:

I look back through the history of the world, of Europe,
and of this country . . . . .and I see a continuum toward
cohesion, comprehensivity, consolidation.

Not a monolithic module.
A singular systematology, its complexity beyond the mere
sum of its sub-group parts

Yes, synergy.
It seems to me.

Oh say, do you see . . . .?

In Forbes magazine, there are often lists of the most prominent and rich people in the world. Reading their names is perhaps the most striking orientation to the success (personal, but each as part of the *system*) of multiculturalism, of nationalistic and racial and religious and sexual diversity. True, some of those achievers came here, recently, pre-proficient. But how many others emerged from a couple generations of just immigrant insignificance still down within the mainstream? Until they achieved prowess and prominence and portfolio etc.

The tangible, resulting synergy?

Communications technology.
Medical procedures including genetics
Music, the art and the business and tech of
Food, the art, prep, proliferation of businesses
Ventures, from the frivolous (pets.com) to profound (research areas noted in previous stuff from me)
Ultra-esoteric R&D (see accompanying page of names involved in brain research (Neurohypophysis).

And another, the final, perspective.
We are all immigrants, members of a prior polyglot pool that
. . . . . prospered **10/19/12**

INDEX

NAME	RANK
Gores, Tom **$2.5 BILLION** PRIVATE EQUITY	159
Gottesman, David **$1.4 BILLION** INVESTMENTS	312
Gottesman, Noam **$1.6 BILLION** HEDGE FUNDS	273
Green, David **$4 BILLION** HOBBY LOBBY	81
Greene, Jeff **$2.1 BILLION** REAL ESTATE, INVESTMENTS	200
Griffin, Ken **$2.3 BILLION** HEDGE FUNDS	171
Gross, Bill **$2.2 BILLION** INVESTMENTS	188
Gustavson, Tamara **$2.3 BILLION** SELF STORAGE	171
Halle, Bruce **$3.4 BILLION** DISCOUNT TIRE	96
Hamm, Harold **$7.5 BILLION** OIL & NATURAL GAS	36
Harris, Joshua **$1.45 BILLION** LEVERAGED BUYOUTS	309
Headington, Timothy **$2.7 BILLION** OIL & GAS, INVESTMENTS	139
Hearst, Austin **$1.9 BILLION** HEARST CORP.	227
Hearst, David Jr. **$1.9 BILLION** HEARST CORP.	227
Hearst, George Jr. **$1.9 BILLION** HEARST CORP.	227
Hearst, William Randolph III **$2.2 BILLION** HEARST CORP.	188
Heisley, Michael Sr. **$1.5 BILLION** MANUFACTURING	293
Hendricks, Diane **$2.2 BILLION** ROOFING	188
Henry, John **$1.1 BILLION** SPORTS	375
Hildebrand, Jeffrey **$5.3 BILLION** OIL	59
Hillman, Henry **$2.2 BILLION** INVESTMENTS	188
Hoffman, Reid **$1.5 BILLION** LINKEDIN	293
Holding, Robert **$2.6 BILLION** OIL, RESORTS	150
Hostetter, Amos Jr. **$2.3 BILLION** CABLE TELEVISION	171
Hubbard, Stanley **$1.9 BILLION** DIRECTV	227
Hughes, Bradley **$1.8 BILLION** SELF STORAGE	242
Huizenga, H. Wayne **$2.3 BILLION** INVESTMENTS	171
Hunt, Johnelle **$1.4 BILLION** TRUCKING	312
Hunt, Ray Lee **$4.3 BILLION** OIL, REAL ESTATE	73
Icahn, Carl **$13 BILLION** LEVERAGED BUYOUTS	25
Ilitch, Michael & Marion & family **$2 BILLION** PIZZA	212
Ingram, Martha & family **$3 BILLION** BOOK DISTRIBUTION, TRANSPORTATION	117
Irsay, James **$1.4 BILLION** INDIANAPOLIS COLTS	312
Jacobs, Irwin **$1.15 BILLION** QUALCOMM	372
Jacobs, Jeremy Sr. **$1.9 BILLION** SPORTS CONCESSIONS	227
Jaharis, Michael **$1.9 BILLION** PHARMACEUTICALS	227
Jamail, Joe Jr. **$1.5 BILLION** LAWSUITS	293
Jannard, James **$3 BILLION** SUNGLASSES	117
Jobs, Steve **$7 BILLION** APPLE, PIXAR	39
Johnson, Abigail **$11.7 BILLION** FIDELITY	29
Johnson, Barbara Piasecka **$3.1 BILLION** JOHNSON & JOHNSON	114
Johnson, Charles **$4.4 BILLION** FINANCIAL SERVICES	72
Johnson, Edward III **$6.5 BILLION** FIDELITY	44
Johnson, H. Fisk **$2.3 BILLION** S.C. JOHNSON & SONS	171
Johnson, Imogene Powers **$2.3 BILLION** S.C. JOHNSON & SONS	171
Johnson, Rupert Jr. **$4.5 BILLION** FRANKLIN RESOURCES	69
Johnson, S. Curtis **$2.3 BILLION** S.C. JOHNSON & SONS	171
Johnson-Leipold, Helen **$2.3 BILLION** S.C. JOHNSON & SONS	171
Johnson-Marquart, Winnie **$2.3 BILLION** S.C. JOHNSON & SONS	171
Jones, Jerry **$1.9 BILLION** DALLAS COWBOYS	227
Jones, Paul Tudor **$3.2 BILLION** HEDGE FUNDS	107
Joseph, George **$1.1 BILLION** INSURANCE	375
Justice, Jim II **$1.1 BILLION** COAL	375
Kaiser, George **$10 BILLION** OIL & GAS, BANKING	31
Kao, Min **$1.8 BILLION** NAVIGATION EQUIPMENT	242
Kaplan, Thomas **$1.8 BILLION** INVESTMENTS	242
Karsh, Bruce **$1.6 BILLION** MONEY MANAGEMENT	273
Keinath, Pauline MacMillan **$2.6 BILLION** CARGILL INC.	150
Kelley, Brad **$1.7 BILLION** TOBACCO	263
Kellogg, Peter **$2.3 BILLION** INVESTMENTS	171
Kennedy, Jim **$6 BILLION** MEDIA	53
Kerkorian, Kirk **$3 BILLION** CASINOS, INVESTMENTS	117
Khosla, Vinod **$1.3 BILLION** VENTURE CAPITAL	331
Kimmel, Sidney **$1.2 BILLION** RETAIL	359
Kinder, Richard **$6.4 BILLION** PIPELINES	46
Kirk, Randal **$2.4 BILLION** PHARMACEUTICALS	166
Knaster, Alexander **$1.1 BILLION** OIL, TELECOM, BANKING	375
Knight, Phil **$13.1 BILLION** NIKE	24
Koch, Charles **$25 BILLION** DIVERSIFIED	4
Koch, David **$25 BILLION** DIVERSIFIED	4
Koch, William **$4 BILLION** OIL, INVESTMENTS	81
Kohler, Herbert Jr. & family **$1.8 BILLION** PLUMBING FIXTURES	242

31. Fincher, K. B., F. W. Bazer, P. J. Hansen, W. W. Thatcher & R. M. Roberts. 198… Proteins secreted by the sheep conceptus suppress induction of uterine prostaglandin F-2α release by oestradiol and oxytocin. J. Reprod. Fertil. 76: 425-433.
32. Sheldrick, E. L. & A. P. F. Flint. 1983. Luteal concentrations of oxytocin decline during early pregnancy in the ewe. J. Reprod. Fertil. 68: 477-480.
33. Flint, A. P. F. & E. L. Sheldrick. 1985. Continuous infusion of oxytocin prevents induction of uterine oxytocin receptor and blocks luteal regression in ewes. J. Reprod. Fertil. 75: 623-631.
34. Sheldrick, E. L. & A. P. F. Flint. 1990. Effect of continuous infusion of oxytocin on prostaglandin $F_{2\alpha}$ secretion and luteolysis in the cyclic ewe. Reprod. Fertil. Dev. 2: 8…-99.
35. Lacroix, M. C., G. Charpigny & P. Reinaud. 1988. Is oxytocin of conceptus origin involved in inhibition of luteal regression in early pregnancy in ewes? J. Endocrinol. 118: R17-R20.
36. Parkinson, T. J., H. J. Stewart, M. G. Hunter, D. S. C. Jones, D. C. Wathes & A. P. F. Flint. 1991. Evidence against a role for blastocyst-secreted oxytocin in early pregnancy maintenance in sheep. J. Endocrinol. 130: 443-449.
37. Vallet, J. L., G. E. Lamming & M. Batten. 1990. Control of endometrial oxytocin receptor and uterine response to oxytocin by progesterone and oestradiol in the ewe. J. Reprod. Fertil. 90: 635-644.
38. Sheldrick, E. L. 1990. Effect of oestradiol-17β on uterine oxytocin receptor synthesis *in vivo* and *in vitro*. J. Reprod. Fertil. Abstr. Ser. 5: 15.
39. E. L. Matthews, V. J. Ayad & D. C. Wathes. 1991. The effect of oestradiol-17β on oxytocin receptor concentration in the reproductive tract of the anoestrous ewe. J. Reprod. Fertil. Abstr. Ser. 8: 81.
40. Lau, T. M., C. B. Gow & R. J. Fairclough. 1992. Increases in the oxytocin-induced prostaglandin $F_{2\alpha}$ response and reduction in the concentrations of endometrial oxytocin receptors in ewes in response to progesterone. J. Reprod. Fertil. 95: 11-18.
41. Sharma, S. C. & R. J. Fitzpatrick. 1974. Effect of oestradiol-17β and oxytocin treatment on prostaglandin F alpha release in the anoestrous ewe. Prostaglandins 6: 97-105.
42. Ayad, V. J., D. C. Wathes, S. A. McGoff & C. L. Gilbert. 1989. Comparison of the actions of oxytocin and [Arg[8]]-vasopressin on the EMG activity of the reproductive tract of oestrogen-treated anoestrous ewes. J. Reprod. Fertil. Abstr. Ser. 4: 26.
43. Leavitt, W. W., W. C. Okulicz, J. A. McCracken, W. Schramm & W. F. Robidoux. 1985. Rapid recovery of nuclear estrogen receptor and oxytocin receptor in the ovine uterus following progesterone withdrawal. J. Steroid Biochem. 22: 687-691.
44. Homanics, G. E. & W. J. Silvia. 1988. Effects of progesterone and estradiol-17β on uterine secretion of prostaglandin $F_{2\alpha}$ in response to oxytocin in ovariectomized ewes. Biol. Reprod. 38: 804-811.
45. Zhang, J., P. G. Weston & J. E. Hixon. 1992. Role of progesterone and oestradiol in the regulation of uterine oxytocin receptors in ewes. J. Reprod. Fertil. 94: 395-404
46. Vallet, J. L. & G. E. Lamming. 1991. Ovine conceptus secretory proteins and bovine recombinant interferon α_1-1 decrease endometrial oxytocin receptor concentrations in cyclic and progesterone-treated ovariectomized ewes. J. Endocrinol. 131: 475-482
47. Sheldrick, E. L. 1991. Oxytocin and luteal maintenance in the ewe. J. Reprod. Fertil. Suppl. 43: 105-107.
48. Sheldrick, E. L. & H. C. Flick-Smith. 1991. Inhibition of ovine endometrial oxytocin receptor synthesis by luteal tissue *in vitro*. J. Endocrinol. 131: Suppl. 84.
49. Abayasekara, D. R. E., E. L. Sheldrick, H. C. Flick-Smith, H. Commander & A. P. F. Flint. 1992. Protein kinase C (PKC) in the sheep endometrium: Mechanism by which interferon (IFN) inhibits oxytocin receptor (OT-R) expression. J. Reprod. Fertil. Abstr. Ser. 9: 65.
50. Godkin, J. D., F. W. Bazer & R. M. Roberts. 1984. Ovine trophoblast protein 1, an early secreted blastocyst protein, binds specifically to uterine endometrium and affects protein synthesis. Endocrinology 114: 120-130.

51 Peterson, A. J., H. R. Tervit, R. J. Fairclough, P. G. Havik & J. F. S… 1976. Jugular levels of 13,14-dihydro-15-keto-prostaglandin F and progesterone … luteolysis and early pregnancy in ewes. Prostaglandins 12: 551-558.
52 Zarco, L., G. H. Stabenfeldt, S. Basu, G. E. Bradford & H. Kindahl. … Modification of prostaglandin F 2α synthesis and release in the ewe during the establishment of pregnancy. J. Reprod. Fertil. 83: 527-536.
53 Gilbert, C. L., P. J. Cripps & D. C. Wathes. 1992. Effect of oxytocin on the p… of electromyographic activity in the oviduct and uterus of the ewe around o… Reprod. Fertil. Dev. 4: 173-203.
54 Ruckebusch, Y. & F. Bayard. 1975. Motility of the oviduct and uterus of th… during the oestrous cycle. J. Reprod. Fertil. 43: 23-32.
55 Garcia-Villar, R., P. L. Toutain, J. More & Y. Ruckebusch. 1982. Spont… motility of the cervix in cyclic and ovariectomized ewes and changes induced by exog… hormones. J. Reprod. Fertil. 66: 317-326.
56 Garcia-Villar, R., P. L. Toutain, D. Schams & Y. Ruckebusch. 1983. Are r… activity episodes of the genital tract controlled by the pulsatile release of oxytocin… Reprod. 29: 1183-1188.
57 Prud'Homme, M. J. 1976. Etude électromyographique de l'organisation de la mo… utérine au cours de l'oestrus chez la brebis. Annls. Biol. Anim. Biochim. Biophy… 821-831.
58 Hunter, R. H. F. 1988. The fallopian tubes: Their role in fertility and infertility. Sp… Verlag. Berlin, Heidelberg, New York.
59 Fuchs, A. R., O. Behrens, H. Helmer, A. Vangsted, M. Ivanisevic, J. Gru… Barros & M. Fields. 1990. Oxytocin and vasopressin binding sites in huma… bovine ovaries. Am. J. Obstet. Gynecol. 163: 1961-1967.
60 Zhang, L., J. J. Dreifuss, M. Dubois-Dauphin & E. Tribollet. 1991. Autoradio… ical localization of oxytocin binding sites in the guinea-pig ovary at different sta… the oestrous cycle. J. Endocrinol. 131: 421-426.
61 Okuda, K., A. Miyamoto, H. Sauerwein, F. J. Schweigert & D. Schams. Evidence for oxytocin receptors in cultured bovine luteal cells. Biol. Reprod. 46: 1007.
62 Sernia, C., R. T. Gemmell & W. G. Thomas. 1989. Oxytocin receptors in the corpus luteum. J. Endocrinol. 121: 117-123.
63 Wathes, D. C. 1984. Possible actions of gonadal oxytocin and vasopressin. J. R… Fertil. 71: 315-345.
64 Wathes, D. C. 1989. Oxytocin and vasopressin in the gonads. *In* Oxford Revi… Reproductive Biology. S. R. Milligan, Ed. Vol. II: 226-283. Oxford University… Oxford, New York, Tokyo.
65 Miyamoto, A. & D. Schams. 1991. Oxytocin stimulates progesterone release from … dialyzed bovine corpus luteum *in vitro*. Biol. Reprod. 44: 1163-1170.
66 Maas, S., H. Jarry, A. Teichmann, W. Rath, W. Kuhn & W. Wuttke. 1992. Par… action of oxytocin, prostaglandin $F_{2\alpha}$ and estradiol within the human corpus lute… Clin. Endocr. Metab. 74: 306-312.
67 Armstrong, D. T. & W. Hansel. 1959. Alteration of the bovine estrous cycle… oxytocin. J. Dairy Sci. 42: 533-542.
68 Wathes, D. C., V. J. Ayad, C. L. Gilbert, S. A. McGoff & C. M. Wathes. Influence of oxytocin infusion during oestrous and the early luteal phase on progest… secretion and the establishment of pregnancy in ewes. J. Reprod. Fertil. 92: 383…
69 Sheldrick, E. L., M. D. Mitchell & A. P. F. Flint. 1980. Delayed luteal regr… in ewes immunized against oxytocin. J. Reprod. Fertil. 59: 37-42.
70 Schams, D., S. Prokopp & D. Barth. 1983. The effect of active and passive immuni… against oxytocin on ovarian cyclicity in ewes. Acta Endocrinol. Copenh. 109: 530…
71 Wathes, D. C., V. J. Ayad, S. A. McGoff & K. L. Morgan. 1989. Effect of… immunization against oxytocin on gonadotrophin secretion and the establishm… pregnancy in the ewe. J. Reprod. Fertil. 86: 653-664.
72 Wathes, D. C., E. L. Matthews & V. J. Ayad. 1992. Effect of oxytocin infusi… secretion of progesterone and luteinizing hormone and the concentration of u…

regarding an article from

PROVIDENTIAL PERSPECTIVE

vol. 26, No. 2, September, 2012 The Teaching Journal of *The Providence Foundation*

Obama, Romney, Other: Who Should Christians Vote for in the 2012 Election?

Including Biblical Qualifications for Civil Leaders

by Stephen McDowell

Herewith, **my** comments.

"Our Founders put us on a Biblical path that enabled us to become the most free, just, prosperous, charitable, and virtuous nation the world has ever seen."

What?? Perhaps Mr. McDowell should read more than his Bible whilst listening to AM radio.

"If any Quaker or Quakers shall presume, after they have once suffered what the law requireth, to come into this jurisdiction . . .every such male Quaker shall for the first offence have one of his ears cut off and be kept at work of correction till he can be sent away at his own charge (cost) and for the second offence (coming into Mass. Bay Colony) shall have his other ear cut off . . . . and every woman Quaker . . .shall be severely whipt. "

A law enacted by those who sought their religious freedom in the new world (but only their way).

Consider how charitable the original distribution of land between those first here: the English, the French, the Spanish. *"Yea, verily as Jesus would have us, let us divide the 'loaf of land' amongst ourselves so that all can be fed with property."*

Consider how justly, how "Jesusly", were treated those to whom this continent had been heritage and home. *"And I say unto thee, any amongst ye who are not of the skin color of ye, ye may send forth from thy midst into the winter of Deer Island even though they profess to have joined the faith of ye."* (Look how charitable and virtuous the "praying Indians" were treated). Most of those thus exiled to that Boston Harbor island

starved or froze to death. The self-protection/self-survival concerns of the settlers (even professing-assimilated Indians a possible subversive, murderous threat) could have been dealt with less cruelly).

Our Founders' original intention was that the rights (including vote) were for those who were male, white, and owners of land. And our Founders so respected the Christian equality of mankind's rights to freedom and pursuit of happiness etc. under God .... unless they happened to be non-male/Protestant/"wealthy" . . . or, especially, owned by someone, including most of our Founders. The recent issue of *Smithsonian* contains an article concerning Jefferson and his slave-ownership (and "co-habitation-ship"). His "moral" reaction to "the peculiar institution" never prevented his owning, even allowing harsh discipline, of this "proto-capitalistic" labor force for his estate and enterprises. But from initial ethical reservations, he eventually realized that slaves, as the product produced by slaves . . provided more profit than his slave-labored agricultural or nail-making enterprises. And he proceeded Capitalistically on that premise.

And the while of these earlier decades, even as European countries quit the trade, America (North and South both) continued this so-profitable, hardly virtuous, commerce . . . . . Biblical?? well, maybe O.T., but surely not within the approbation of Jesus and the N. T.

Ongoing while the black skin population increased to pretty-much self-replication without further expense for importation . . . the red skin bunch were not really prospering under, at this point, subsequent leaders of this *"most free, just, . . .charitable, and virtuous nation"*. This continent was populated by "Indians" at the beginning of the 19th century. By the end, essentially a genocide had been committed (involving battle-related massacres, but also ethnic-cleansing forages rewarded by differential payments to the white "settlers" (or other) for male, female, or child scalp. (The attrition/wipeout was from some few millions of aboriginal peoples to a final @250,000, herded from their homeland to the "proto-concentration camps" called reservations.

How Nazi, not Christian!!!!

NEW YORK -- EARLY SOCIOECONOMIC STATUS

Almost daily involvement by law enforcement with runaway indentured servants or apprentices escaping abuse

"Ann Sewall savagely beat Ann Parsons and kept her in chains and irons for several weeks upon bread and water only."

". . .Brughman had so disfigured [his servant's] face that he stood in danger of losing his eyes."

Numerous bawdy houses (gin mills, prostitution, traffic in stolen goods, etc. and catering to all classes and even Negroes.

Many run in their houses by unmarried women unable to earn a living otherwise.

1730 census: 8,622 7,045 whites 1,577 blacks

@140 merchants and landowners held almost half taxable wealth

49% of whites held prop. worth ten pounds or less

Thus @ 1/3 of all whites were destitute

Blacks worse off, of course

"All . .Negroes as shall be found to be assembled -- & if any of them refuse to submit, then fire upon them, kill or destroy them . . ." (edict in response to Negro unrest)

Two years later, prominent landowner tries to prevent his slaves from going to Sabbath services and killed along with his wife and 5 children by slave Sam and wife, who were quickly apprehended. Sam impaled and hung in chains. Wife burned alive. [this is New York . . in America . . !!]

Servile rebellion in 1712, quickly put down

6 conspirators killed themselves
20 hanged
3 burned to death, one by slow roasting
1 hung in chains without sustinence until dead
1 "broken alive upon a wheel" . .(his bones broken, one by one, over a period of hours by a bar)

"The real legacy of the 1712 uprising was a new era of routinized brutality and official cynicism toward slaves. Crowds of townsfolk often gathered now to watch slaves hanged or burned to death for one offence or another." Female slave whipped, dragged by cart, whipped again for talking to a white. Male slave whipped to death for "being on the streets at night".

So Christian, so Jesus-like, the mid-and-onward into early 20th century welcome *(kind of "let the children of other nations come unto me")* welcome of the Irish, Italians, Southern European and Eastward Jews. So virtuous and charitable the conditions in New York City where burnings-alive, even breakings-on-wheel took place, where the filth piled save for what the roaming pigs ate, where people lived in tenements, the basements of which would be intermittently flooded by overflowing privies in the back yards -- yet a prominent Protestant church (I think Trinity) was one of the major property owners. And so obvious the God-blessed absence of any cursed socialistic-sin that would have taken from the ultra-rich (one of whom spent millions on his daughter's NY wedding), another whose daughter's betrothal to European nobility required a "dowry" of millions allocated to the refurbishment of Blenheim.

Gee, isn't there something in the Bible about a rich man not having much chance of getting into heaven?

Gee, can't you picture it? Jesus. Bread. The crowd beyond. And Jesus did break the bread and maybe one of the disciples said something socialistic like, *"I think some of these people are hungry"*. And Jesus broke the bread and rebuked Barack and saith unto him and the others, *"This is Capital expansion, profit. We can make a fortune on "food-stuff alchemy" that it seems I'm able to do. This'll work with fishes too!! We got the potential for a mass market here, guys. As for those people, why aren't they working rather than hanging around out here? We don't need no welfare state . . . ."*

Or picture the old lady with the coin and she's about to put it in . . .

"STOP!!!!!" That's your wealth. Which isn't really a significant wealth. But at least you have the potential to invest it to get some kind of dividend, some time hence with a dot.com a quick cash-out share appreciation (who cares if there's ever any actual cash flow??) Keep your wealth. God wants you to not distribute."

And having left historic New York . . .we come to more recent Washington.

Ah, Ronald Reagan. The Man of God. Kind of a quasi-cousin to Jesus, the Son of God? Reagan *thought we were going "in the wrong direction and attempted to change course"*.

To a considerable extent, Reaganomics may have represented the true first fruition of the credit-based bubble that finally burst so recently. Sure, things took off and boomed and people worked and earned and bought and bought more than they earned (on credit) so there could be even more manufacture and production than the actual, substantive basis of a market stability. Also, this was still the era of post-WWII development of devices and technologies. Also increase of population.

As for "trickle-down"? Seems somewhat a restriction of necessary monetary flow into the vast pool of . . . consumer-demographic!! Which means the vast population of lower income people who purchase things and services and stuff otherwise. The operant obverse of "trickle-down" is "held-up" economics, yes rewarding ambition and innovation and even exploitation and greed (which are absolutely necessary components of a successful socio-economic system . . . and I'll use the term "Darwinian" too. How obviously from history, absolute socialism, especially Communism, doesn't work. Aspiration and competition and reward are indispensable).

But when "trickle-down" allows multi-million dollar *incomes* to be so disproportionately retained (relative to the nothing that's left for the vast majority to be able to save, let alone horde) . . . . the while schools are without supplies, parks are untended, police and firemen laid off, libraries closed, millions without health care, sporadic areas of actual malnutrition . . . . . it's not only un-Christian!!! It sucks the sustenance out of the broad economic system (enterprises and jobs).

The vast wealth "held-up" primarily circulates only in the "high-end" high end.

Biblical? Christian?

"Thou shalt beat thy plows into sword-shares". * No cuts of military budget.

Get rid of all the myriad "socialistic" programs that this country has established in order to provide for its *"people, the sheep of its pastures"*, so to speak. The list of Mitt's intended cuts and deletions represents a flaying of the flesh, a disembowelment of the organism, of what America has come to represent as a Christian concept nation. This "concept" obviously includes feeding the hungry, clothing the naked, healing the sick, "Samaritanish" stuff to help others. Educating the children. Providing for the security of the elderly. Etc. Etc. Etc. *Mitt's a Joel man (3:10) -- not an Isaiah (2:4) or Micah (4:3).

So, if anyone gets his subsidy or assistance reduced, he should compensate for the loss with dividend income or share-price increment cash-in. Buy military-industrial-complex stock!!!!

How crippling, FDR's polio. Worse, his "sincialistic" (sinful-socialistic) programs such as social security!! Wouldn't we be so much better off had Deuteronomy 1:13 been heeded *("Choose wise and discerning and experienced men")*, and as advocated, instead of Social Security (such Satanistic sin), all had put all into Wall Street?

Notwithstanding the OT entitlement *"have dominion over"* and mandate *"go forth and subdue"*, it seems that Biblical, especially Christian Biblical requirement would be that man respect, preserve, maintain that which God has provided him. Such just might include the earth upon which he lives. Its resources as treasures, not quick-buck mass-market products for exploitation, excess utilization, and conversion to waste and pollution.

So virtuous our Founding Fathers and those who followed in their *footprints* upon the ethnic-cleansed, clear-cut, crop-depleted, super-fund-polluted, even riparian-combustive (several cases) desecration of what God hath created.

The "performance of recitation or ritual or such" or the "alarmism of approaching Armageddon" -- are these the criteria of being God-loving or God-fearing? Is the adherence to the specific schism's self-sanctity-assumption to be "of God" the requisite for really being "of God"? Thus, the Catholic is not Godly to the Protestant but the Methodist is not to the Baptist but the Lutheran is not to the Pentacostal but the other Evangelical is not Godly to the ..... and of course, the Jews are out of the God-loop entirely except where Israel represents a sort of "1st nation" logistical preemption over all others; also in their own self-to-God relationship-primacy-assumption.

Mitt will drill, baby, drill. On the land and on the sea.

Great idea. And God saith, *"suck all that oil out, and the coal, the Nat'l gas. Get it soon as you can because that'll make jobs for people because jobs pay wages and wages go into the free market system which is my other $pecial Creation from which profits derive and investor portfolios expand and many (though the few) get richer and richer"*.

Great idea to use up our resource reserves (projected to last for the next 200 years!!! -- hardly more than 2 generations). These have proven means for extraction (drill, frack, etc.) and conversion into fuels. Perhaps these should remain as our reserves? And in the meantime we should, along with the other countries in the world, participate in using up each others'? And, collaboratively, invent and implement alternatives!!

Or should we introduce a Monroe Doctrine "circuit-breaker" system/syndrome on any and all internationalism, even though that's now a "set" of which *domesticism (American market/economy)* is but a subset?

Great idea to vastly expand the availability of finite resources to lower the price so more people will use more so it will be used up in even less time. And meanwhile we'll stop buying from those other countries (such as OPEC) and when our revenues for their oil no longer provide an income to their nations they'll love us the more, respecting our self-sufficiency, autonomy, independence, cessation of their survival $ource . . . ?

Mitt's going to build that pipeline. Right over an aquifer, I believe. What the hell, what's to worry about water when it would cost more to re-route the oil (which I understand to be the main opposition -- the route of the pipe). But we need to get right on it. Not wait. For with some (is it) 23 million people out of work, between the oil rigs and the pipe line we'll get them all back on the job. . . . . . .??

Mitt. Multi-millionaire. Obviously thus in a position to network, combine, collaborate, joint-venture with others of that echelon.

Mitt. Market forces man. Get demon government out of things. Saint Private Sector solely and singly for salvation.

Mitt. Why is it that he's not done, and is not doing *anything*, in the private paradigm? He does nothing until/unless he becomes the head of . . .***the government***??? Remember, the Bush tax cuts, which Mitt wants to retain *in toto*, have been in place *"providing tax relief and incentive for business investment to grow our economy"* . . . for how long? Part of Bush & since, thru almost 4 years of Obama. Where are the jobs?? There ought to be jobs. But I see only clowns.

Except for increased drilling off- and onshore (including wildlife refuges), where will all the jobs come from? Back from? Will that be it? "Re-shoring" of manufacturing and assembling and all to America's shores? China and so many other countries have become co-dependent on globalism-as-détente (as well as their in**tra**-national security-through-employment plus prosperity to some extent apportioned to keep their populations peaceful). Even if we could pull back our jobs to our population, might our position be worsened by depriving, devaluing, depressing, even desecrating these other populations?

Might our national security become far less secure, because having lost what they were reciprocating with us, what would other countries (or their terrorist proxies) have to lose by attacking us?

Or would those then literally starving (because peasantry is passe as possibility for all in those lands) . . .would they respect us for assuming self-sufficiency and ceasing sinful, socialistic *"global distribution of jobs, thus survival paradigm?"*

As for China stealing? Yes, no doubt espionage and "pirating" and Intel. Prop. theft goes on. But by the cheap labor there (and in all those other countries), the corporations of here not only sell more (because they can sell cheap), but the profits percolate up into dividends and exorbitant remunerations.

But since we can't put millions to work drilling or pipe-fitting . . .

Unto Walmart (and Apple and you-name-it-everything-else), Mitt saith, *"Thou shalt bring thy jobs back to America. And thou shalt pay thy people here enough that they can maintain their life- and indulgence/purchase-style and consume great quantities of pumped productivity!!!"*

Aside from it's being also impossible, it would be consumer-sided self-destructive were he to offer as incentive to the Prodigal Sons of Corporate Cavorting abroad . . . . *"If thee return to thy home and honor thy family [domestic labor] I'll make it so it doesn't cost you any more than you're paying over there."*

Yeah, maybe some corporations would come on home (likely only if the government paid for the relocation costs) -- except that the wages wouldn't be sufficient for the producers to become consumers who could pay for the production.

Picture that Escher drawing of two hands kind of drawing each other. Now picture the hands holding, not pencils inscribing, but erasers . . . .

Get it?? As it "depicts" what would happen to the economy??

Regarding: (from the article)

Faith or True Religion -- "men who fear God" and a couple other items

I'll make a couple comments.

"April 2008 -- Obama speaks disrespectfully of Christians, saying they 'cling to guns or religion' and have an 'antipathy to people who are not like them'."

Obama was not speaking of Christians -- rather, a segment or demographic thereof which just might include some Catholics (which in any other context the "Christians" so offended by Obama's statement . . .wouldn't consider as "Christian"). Obama was not demeaning Christianity. Nor can it be presumed that his sole focus was on gun-owning or religiousness.

Included in his referent-group were not well-off, religious people (maybe we could include even Cheney . . .and many others of the high-end who not only hunt, but collect "precious weapons" and go on safaris as well as to church!!

Barack was, very inadvisedly, pointing out a demographic that <u>does have antipathy</u>

towards people who are not like them, and for whom just being armed (with bullets or Bible) seems to be essential *raison d'etre*, if not metabolism!!

April 2009 . . . Jesus's name was covered when he (Obama) was making a speech

Possibly this was a factor of Homeland Security? Think about that! Those in the murderous parts of the world watch TV too. Would it really be wise to "visually conflate" the faith of the Crusaders (even recent -- as seen by them) with the President of a supposedly church-and-state-separate nation? For what purpose what would appear a flaunt or provocation, if not identifying the nation's head with a religion they hold as Satanic? Is the icon, the emblem, the logo, the symbol, so much required? So sacred? What about the heart and soul of the self (selves) of Christian believers as sufficient? Or is the symbol, a depiction, more sacred to the sensitive (kind of like representations of "the Prophet" to those others . . .)?

The insinuation that Obama is a Muslim-in-disguise is absurd. That he belonged to Rev. Wright's rabid-sermoned church is because, though mixed-race, Barack associates himself with "black", and blacks are into that kind of fire and brimstone ("an' we suffered it personally heaped upon us during slavery") displacement? No, ***catharsis*** of "race-heritage-rage". (Long after slavery ended, there was the KKK and Jim Crow, the lynching continued, not legislatively ended until, I believe, the 1950s. So Christian and in all ways virtuous this land of the free-for-all freedom-fight for so long. Interesting, the Southern Democrats for a long time blocked attempts to pass legislation against lynching!!

February 2012 - apologizing for Koran burnings was at least a wise attempt (although it doesn't seem the apology was really accepted by the apologizee), the rabid, rampant, Muslim "street". Here was, again, perhaps another nuance of not only homeland security, but for our "those-over-there", an attempted amelioration of situation -- by trying to calm psychotic reaction of their (Muslims) those-over-there.

That we burn Bibles here? Well, (Escher, above was the first), let's look at a second very convolute comparison, perhaps inside-out analogy. In other countries people burn our flag. Though we don't rampage, we get very upset. (Our burning their Korans seemed to them like their burning our flag to us. Kind of equal but opposite offended -- despite the drastically different degree of response.) But consider that in official flag-protocol, we burn "retired" flags. And, I've learned from this article, Bibles. We approve. No problem.

But where there is such out-of-control syndrome as Islamophrenia?

Obama offered an apology for offending their faith.

What's wrong with that?

Seems more Christian than not doing so.

A mere gesture, in part to subdue threat to our personnel abroad.

Barack said, "sorry" . . . to a "them" . . .
Jesus even invoked God's forgiveness of . . . another . . . . "them" .

Homosexuality has always been, will always be. There was a time when it posed a national threat. Sexuality/reproduction represented the organic-military-industrial complex (human reproduction -- of males). Engaging in sex taking time, and energy-consuming, but yielding **no product** (boy-babies to become soldiers eventually) compromised the MIC. (The time I refer to was Biblical and later historic eras). Another factor for the hetero-fixation was transmission of personal bloodlines and property through progeny. Procreation was priority over pleasurable permutations.

Homosexual "infrastructure" is an organic inherent. All creatures (that includes humans) are <u>conceived</u> female. Only after a period of cell-differentiating gestation, a binary dynamic of chromosomal "hardware" -- and hormonal-chemical "software" (uterine and circulatory milieu) -- does the unborn "potential" proceed as actualized male or female gender, at least as obvious overt morphology of genitalia and inside repro organs (although there are variations and exceptions from "mainstream" m or f.)

Homosexual as "infra-chemical" being? Male and female both have male and female hormones, the proportions (testosterone, estrogen, and others) quite variable. Despite morphologically indisputable one-or-the-other-ness, the level (including "proprioception" of one's maleness or femaleness) can vary, be ambivalent, bi, or homo.

Whichever and whatever, is there not something else in the Bible about God being the one to judge, Judgment (ultimate) being up to HIM? If enacting homosexuality a sin of life-style choice, God will not only have to punish an awful lot of people (including some prominent evangelists and we won't mention priests) . . . . but other species. For homosexual behavior occurs all through the various forms of life, specially "created", . . or through God's most comprehensive and amazing special creation -- evolution's miraculous materialization of God's *system*.

As for homosexual marriage? That someone would fear it might lead the otherwise heterosexual person away from male-and-female union . . . maybe that's someone's subconscious recognition of *his* inherent potential . . . . . historical perspective reveals, "hardly". Man and woman will mate. The while, there may be all kinds of combinations and permutations. But marriage is not under threat. Nor will youth be converted-*subverted-perverted* to homo-lifestyle. Homosexuality is not a religion let alone cult.

But I do not approve of homosexual "marriage". From the basis of keeping the <u>language</u> from being at least *diverted*! "Marriage" has meant man and woman for eons. So keep it that way and get another term for the love, caring, creating, exploring, existing . . of man-man or woman-woman . . . **unions**.

Thus, a why not for "marriage" . . . somewhat analogous (oh my god, here I go again), to a why not for Blacks achieving equality but clamoring that that's not good enough. "We don't just want equal rights. We want to be called Caucasians!"

And why would anyone want to use the term "Marriage?" Such a fallible institution (almost 1/3 fail within the first six years, I believe. Heterosexual marriages. Hardly sacred, "til-death-do-us-part perpetuity!!!

I do agree with a few points in the article regarding rights of religious decisions.

Hiring and health matters -- some decisions should not be superimposed. Along with the right to privacy there should be the right to priorities: even in some cases discriminatory. Catholic hospitals should not have to deal with contraception, let alone anything abortive. Certain organizations should not have to provide equal-opportunity to unwanted beliefs or orientations (although we see how uneffective even the Boy Scouts have been in self-regulating prohibitions of anyone homosexual from their Physically Pure and Morally Straight organization. But failure to achieve doesn't justify subjection to superimpositions usurping *intentions*. Some places the government does need to back-off.

Finally I come to . . . life

Protestant lifers propound that life begins at conception.

Catholic doctrine, however, starts a bit earlier and considers that *preventing* conception is sin!!

But aren't they a little late in the system of reproductive components?

Wouldn't male nocturnal emissions be . . . sins? Partial-murder? Pre-penetration abortion?

And, of course, menstruation destroys ovum (sometimes -a). SIN!!

All the uproar and outcry about the unborn, the pre-conscious (even if "*sentient*", a state prior to agony's affliction) such as . . .

starvation . . . . .

disease . . . . . .

sexual slavery to lunatic warlords. . . . .

potential recruits in their thousands, the orphans of Africa, for organization by Alqaida)

Oh, but people would have to give more or actually do something
or **go** somewhere and it's so much easier just holding up signs .....
about the sanctity of life, the salvation of the unborn

but again I ask . . .

what
about

THE

BORN ?

Regarding **your** oil (if the source and resource were personally yours)

Points to ponder.

My term "oil" here is a generic which includes
not only petroleum, but gas, and also
the various "geologic containments" (shale, etc.)

You buy and sell oil from a global market combining specific
resources of Canada, Norway, Venezuela, Africa,
OPEC, U. S. (already), and more.

From the oil you buy, you sell branded petroleum products and are making "windfall profits".

You have oil under **your** (own) land – land which you also farm.

You already drill, pump, and significantly profit from your "domestic" reserves – your own oil resource and source.

Your agricultural activities and survival otherwise depend upon the purity, even potability, of the water under your land.

Obviously, you're aware that drilling, fracking, etc. entail risk of Leaks or other contamination of the land and underlying aquifer/wells. You have only so much oil under your land. One projection is 100 years' reserve. That would take care of two generations' of your lineage.

You should: 1)

Drill and pump as much of your own oil as fast as you can so that it can be sold cheaper and thus consumed faster especially as gasoline in automobiles.

Sell this "domestic" reserve into the International petro-pool, thus lowering market prices so that the burgeoning consumer masses of China and India (and soon, elsewhere) can use more and more and more of everyone's oil reserves

You should: 2)

I think, obviously, do neither of the above. Bad enough with mere products, but to advocate increasing production for the sake of stimulating more consumption . . of any natural resource . . . is akin to anarchy!! As for lower price as proportionate to pumping volume or specific source . . . . . . hah.

Re. another email

First, summary of last: "Your own oil" – one of last week's emails.
Instead of oil, think of the commodity as food. You only have so much.
You depend on your supply for your survival, and for monetary profit.
Would you lower the price in order to sell a lot more in a hurry and thus, the sooner, use up the limited supply you have?
Given alternative "routes", would you insist upon running a pipeline across your food-source, knowing the chance of leakage? Remember, "footprints" such as the little Valdez in the great big ocean and the Tiny-er BP drilling rig in the Carribean . . . . footprings "BLEED" . . . . (Under the contested pipeline route is a major aquifer)
The "conservatives' " compulsion to drill, drill, drill is but one of the many areas of advocating exploitation of the irreplaceable, for the sake of mere monetary (and momentary) gain

And now, to the first of this weekend's . . . .

Concerning Alternative Energy (by AHSchneider)

There are several fuels/systems being researched/developed
Solar, wind, wave, plant-based, algae-based, hydrogen cell and even others I'd term "esoterics"

No one of these will likely ever provide for even **all** the *stationary* electrical needs of developed countries, let alone providing charge for mobile electrical demands (cars, trucks).

Even the combination of all these may not suffice for heavy industrial demands (such as smelting, electroplating, production welding, and large electric motor-powered manufacturing or mining processes.

At present, solar and wind seem to be viable systems for limited power generation – but the costs associated are greater than for petro- or gas-fueled generating facilities.

There is no *certainty* that wave, algae, even fuel cell energy derivation will become market-feasible.

There may always be "conventional grid" electrical requirements for the population, not just for its industry and production demands. So there may be an open-ended time frame in which petroleum or gas resources are of ultimate and absolute necessity.

Given that "foreign oil" is part of what the U.S. uses may be part of why the price is high.

Paying OPEC countries for oil is like indulging the (Islamic) enemy.

Not exploiting all our domestic reserves in order to provide our people with cheap automotive fuel so they can use more by traveling more . . . is unpatriotic, anti-capitalistic.

We should: 1)

Mourn that Newt Gingrich didn't get his chance to lower the price of gasoline to $2.50-something a gallon so everyone could splurge on consumption, within a couple generations use ours up all of ours.

Shut off OPEC oil. That way we'll be so much safer when the rulers no longer have our petro-wealth and our "proxy-protection" . . . and the populace, thus reduced to actual starvation, would have even more rabid reasons to attack us

Make sure whoever we elect will disregard all the treasonous "market-globalism" and also the nonsense about our domestic environment and drill and frack all the oil and gas wherever it is and whatever the result because it'll boost consumption thus lower price (supply-demand ratio). And put people to work. A few. For little while.

Make sure that even sequential venture capital funding is allocated to start-ups of shoe-sales, coffee-shops, hamburger chains, boutique wine-sample websites, and such. Profit-taking from share-value increments of such "second-wave dot.coms" make any matter of eventual cash-flow rather secondary in the paradigm of investment-to-return priority for the in-group who know when to bail out.

Don't back "boondoggles" like Solectra or Evergreen Solar, with combined VC, or (heaven forbid) any government subsidy to keep the industries and jobs in this country through the development period

until they'd achieve self-sustaining financial state. And such potential strategic survival industries (as opposed to subs and sips, etc.) present the possibility of becoming major employers.

As for biofuels etc., conservatives view such innovations as imaginations' delusions.

As stated in Forbes Mag.. . . "we live in a world or oil . . . ."

. . . . projections are
for 100 years' domestic reserves (U.S.) – and
as said above, that's only 2 generations.
Then what?

But (concluding 1),

We should use all of ours. Drill, buy, and burn American!!! When our supply has been depleted we don't have to worry about from whom will come our energy resources. We'll be dead then. Screw the future. Even our great-grand children. After all, what did any of them ever do for us???

But seriously

Or we should: 2)

Realize that some alternatives may not ever be viable.
That even all alternatives may not provide all needs
That we may always need to draw from whatever petroleum/gas sources are available.

Realize that we have resource-reserves, and proven means to drill, frack, and otherwise extract – and to process into fuels and other petro-chemical products

Realize that we should by all means preserve our safety:

By preserving **our own** resources for the future. For now, we should continue drawing from the multi-nation petro-pool..

By maintaining a politico-economic/détente reciprocity with OPEC, and even Mr. Chavez.

By actually providing for the survival, if not also the semi-Westernization, of OPEC-country populace through our petro-presence of (personnel other than Arab, and the concommitant subtle "insurgence" of Western culture). . . . as well as the $$$s.

Conclusion: don't blow through your own by making it cheap and then you got no choice, let alone control, over the other guys' resources!!!!!!

Regarding the Middle East's oil.

Part of the "foreign oil" America uses comes from OPEC.
OPEC nations are Islamic, thus consider Christianity a blasphemy, denounce democracy as a heresy.
Blasphemy and heresy are Satanic and the destruction of their adherents will be rewarded. Such is the view of many Islamic fundamentalists, even the quest of extremists. *And for oil we pay money to them*???

Almost all of the revenue of the OPEC countries comes from oil
The drilling/extraction of that oil, as well as significant (if not pre-ponderant) revenue derives from Western (incl. American) petrochemical companies and Western nation consumption of refined petro-products.

The distribution of OPEC revenue provides extreme, ostentatious wealth for the elite, while leaving the vast majority of the population rather, if not actually, impoverished, suppressed, unemployed, and worse.

Thus the Mideast kingdoms and their myriad privileges and princes depend upon a Western presence, not only petro-financially, but "existentially". The West is both potential protector from popular uprising and provision of funds for protracted, projected dynastic enrichment.

What "trickle-down" economic enhancement provides for the populace derives from Western capital infusion for oil extraction.

Payments to OPEC are a *quid pro quo* for that aspect of popular suppression (by royalty) which protects Western petrochemical facilities and equipment, as well as product. Termination of Western capital into

OPEC would end our collusion with their ruling echelon, further impoverish their people (think Iraqi sanctions), and result in revved rage readings (religious and otherwise).

Cessation of Western payments for, and usage of, OPEC oil would result in replacing the prevalent infusion from, influence by, and power (geo-political and potential military) of other countries such as Russia, China . . . even India.

Therefore, to resolve any dilemma regarding OPEC oil . . . .

We should: 1)

Stop trading with bastards that don't like us and our religion and show them how much they need us and are helpless (or hopeless) without us. (What else would Jesus do??)

Use up all our reserves first, for we alone will set the price so much cheaper and thus enable such increased usage for such factorial short-term profits.

Thus postpone eventual need to resume OPEC derivation/ extraction which Russia and China and even India will have exploited fully . . . . but of course will share so cooperatively with us . . . .with U. S.

We should: 2)

Do none of the above.

We should continue the present paradigm of oil production, propping-up and proxy-postulate positioning of emirates (etc.), populace/extremist controls, etc. as we have been for years.

For in the Middle East, our presence and even our payments represent an investment in a global-domain socio-politi-economic conflation of control, thus their, and our, national security.

The petro-resources derived are actually but the "interest" we derive from that kind of globalized-investment portfolio.

We might "profit" more . . . . . but at what cost?

Regarding Netanyahu's speech and the rest of the material that follows below my commentary:

As Naziism showed, even a minority "echelon" can become the "movement" of a whole population. And though the majority of Muslim people may just be followers of Islamic religious (and dietary) practices, there is that sinister, potentially catalytic core of socio-atavistic/philoso-genocidal extremists who could become the SS of the Prophet.

But to terminate by force Iran's nuclear program seems almost beside the point.

"Termination" would probably (as with Iraq) be just postponement and relocation.

Destroying centrifuges and such might be no more efficacious in removing existential threat to Israel than our flushing Alqaeda and others out of the caves of Afghanistan, There, they were "contained" and surveilled significantly. Iran is not only such a "containment", but also a developed nation, civilization, economy, etc. Iran actually faces its own existential threat, were it to initiate any enactment of Ama*dimwit*jad's bluster. (and he is even at some odds with the clerics who actually seem to run the place).

Disrupting a nation's nastinesses might take the least of the nasties out of things. Far from Iran's being nuclear comparable to Alqaeda, terrorists are out and out such, without any mitigating interests or agendas, even their own survival. Iran is a country with survival-interests, if not priority!!

I do not see a nation assuming advantage by becoming a suicide-bomber.

I do see that if actual terrorists were to be provided access to nuclear anything (from uranium up to a complete weapon), there are "markets" such as North Korea, Pakistan, and an almost international-spread and span of arms-dealings and dealers, deliveries.

My perspective is that the Middle East is a potential "religious Reich" and a preemptive attack on one part, could well create a fusion-reaction of the whole region: Sunnis and Shiites and some Kurds and Wheys and whatevers all joined hand in hand under the banner of ISLAM -- also their nations' survival vs. the Western degeneracy, debauchery, displaced "manifest destiny".

The observed perspective seems to be that by getting rid of even secular despots, Islamic extremists and Brotherhoods etc. take the place of somewhat malleable individuals -- with the mania of Islamic movements (sects, groups, etc.)

As for reference to the Soviet Union, perhaps far more salient a consideration is what would have resulted had the US (or even a "coalition of the other-side-of-the-curtain" had launched actual military action vs. Russia's armaments, silos, and such?

A highly important and significant term, concept, status, policy here: DETENTE

Even, or especially, when MAD is involved (mutually assured destruction). The downfall of the Soviets was brought about, in part by the bipart nuclear proliferation, theirs and ours, which they ultimately could not afford to continue. Regarding Kennedy, there was a trade-off for Kruschev's removal from Cuba and our taking back missiles from somewhere or other in Europe. A *mutual* retreat from MAD.

If Iran actually, not just preemptively, but even retributively, attacked Israel, Iran would case to be a nation and at that point, given "pasha-proliferation", a lot of the whole region would be laid waste.

For Israel at least, likely many others, would hold back nothing to destroy destroyers. For Israel then would be backed by, essentially, world's war forces.

But there are other countries with interests and influences (and actually the provision of Israel's protections, military per se and "backup". And Iran's far-from-dear-leader (and a whole political dimension different from a Hitler), even he must well recognize that Israel itself is hardly the threat. For Israel is the proxy (and only up to a point) personnel of the West.

The West could become a real big multi-national conglomerate conquerer..

Considering what the Jewish people have gone through through the centuries, even paranoia may be preventive/preemptive wisdom. But the syndrome of simplistic strike first to cease threat -- *is* simplistic given the anti-West, anti-Israel, anti-Christian unsurveilled network of proliferant or variant existential exterminants -- such as those weapons that Alqaeda or the others could get on the open arms market.

But why bother?

I'm sure Israel depends on a rather "contained" source of water, reservoir, wells, ...

But . . . aside from all the above, if Netanyahu (*et.* govt. or military coalition) really want to do an erasure before the actual red line is drawn, it certainly can be done. We're not going to disarm them (Israel) as prevention, or would we thereafter -- nor have we in the past even to prevent their enacting even what our broader interests and inferences, might have deemed dangerous or even self-destructive.

On Sep 27, 2012, at 8:06 PM, CJUI - Christians and Jews United for Israel wrote:

Christians and Jews in defense of Israel and of liberty and Judeo-Christian values in America

Netanyahu's Speech at U.N.

September 27, 2012

NRG: Netanyahu's Speech - Transcript and Summary by BreitBart

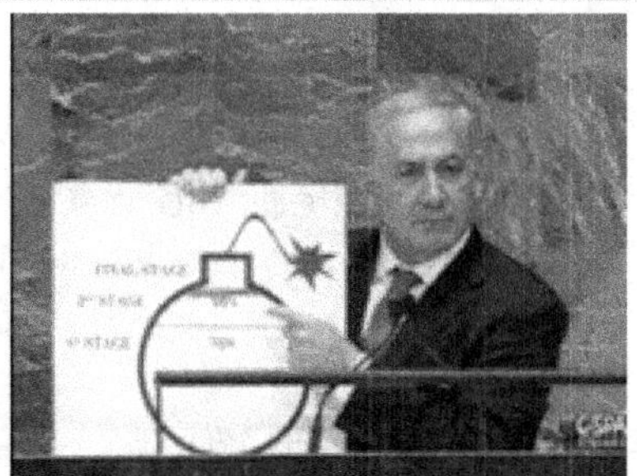

Netanyahu Draws 'Red Line' for Obama

by Ben Shapiro, Breitbart, 9/27/2012

This afternoon, Israeli Prime Minister Benjamin Netanyahu took to the podium at the General Assembly of the United Nations - and once again, he gave an impassioned speech outlining the history and values of the Jewish State, and explaining in perfectly basic terms what the West's "red line" should be with regard to Iranian nuclear development.

Netanyahu began his speech by putting the State of Israel's existence in historic context. Fighting back against Iranian president Mahmoud Ahmadinejad's smear that the Jews have no real history in Israel, Netanyahu talked about the Jews' 3,000 year history in the land. "The Jewish State will live forever," he said defiantly. "The Jewish people have come home. We will never be uprooted again."

Netanyahu then attacked the battle of ideologies that has culminated in the current standoff with an Iranian regime bent on destruction of Israel. The battle, he said, was "modern versus the medieval." "These forces clash around the world," said Netanyahu. He continued:

The medieval forces of radical Islam whom you just saw storming the American embassies throughout the Middle East, well, they oppose this. They seek supremacy over all Muslims. They're bent on world conquest. They want to destroy Israel, Europe, America. They want to extinguish freedom. They want to end the modern world.

Now, militant Islam has many branches, from the rulers of Iran with their Revolutionary Guards to al-Qaida terrorists to the radical cells lurking in every part of the globe.

But despite their differences, they are all rooted in the same bitter soil of intolerance. That intolerance is directed first to their fellow Muslims and then to Christians, Jews, Buddhists, Hindus, secular people, anyone who doesn't submit to their unforgiving creed. They want to drag humanity back to an age of unquestioning dogma, unrelenting conflict.

I'm sure of one thing. Ultimately, they will fail. Ultimately, light will penetrate the darkness.

He added that Palestinian leader Mahmoud Abbas' "libelous" language about Israel did not forward the peace process.

Then Netanyahu got to the meat of the matter. A nuclear-armed Iran, said Netanyahu, would be analogous to a nuclear-armed al Qaeda. "Given this record of Iranian aggression without nuclear weapons ... imagine them with nuclear weapons," he said. Diplomacy, Netanyahu noted, had failed. More than that, diplomacy had granted Iran an additional period to complete its nuclear development.

What the West needs, Netanyahu said, is a "clear red line" with regard to "one vital part of [Iran's] program and it's the nuclear enrichment program." He explained why the world needed a red line:

Red lines don't lead to war. Red lines prevent war. Just look at NATO's charter. It made clear that an attack on one member country would be considered an attack on all, and NATO's red line helped keep the peace in Europe for nearly half a century. President Kennedy set a red line during the Cuban missile crisis. That red line also prevented war and helped preserve the peace for decades.

In fact, it's the failure to place red lines that's often invited aggression.

He went directly at the Obama-created myth that Iran is a small country with little power, stating that Iran is bigger than Great Britain, Germany, France and Italy "combined."

Then came the most controversial portion of Netanyahu's speech. He pulled out a cartoon diagram of a bomb, divided into three stages: 70% uranium development, 90% uranium development, and final stage development. He then pulled out a red marker and drew a clear line before final stage development. The "red line," he said, should be drawn before that "final stage." And, he added, "every day, that point is getting closer."

The leftist media has pounced on Bibi's cartoon of the bomb - but the fact remains that it was a clear and understandable image for the American public. More than that, it was an unmistakable signal to the Obama administration that if they insist on acting ignorant, Netanyahu will treat them as such, as he should. Netanyahu's muscular defense of Israel and his bravery in elucidating the basic civilizational conflict at work in the Middle East has set the table for a decision by the West. The only question now is: will Obama continue to shilly-shally on Iran, even as they draw closer to achieving their promised nuclear Holocaust?

(from a friend, in response to an email from me.)

Exploiting our own energy resources may finally free us from our current malaise. Far vaster than could recently have been imagined, we can at last envision energy independence (in concert with the rest of N America) within a few years. From this many blessings will flow: freedom from mid-east entanglements and corresponding lessening of military needs, reduced trade imbalance from this plus export biz, reduced carbon emissions, jobs, revenue from taxes and royalties, lowered costs to citizens, etc.

Gee, I would think you'd be leading the cheers, but apparently not...

(and my response to him)

I interpret just the opposite. Our global petro-sources represent part of the global economy, providing survival *income* for other countries, probably most of which comes back to us through their purchases of Western commodities (of course including high-end cars etc. for their elite .. . . and mega-millions for weaponry from our M. I. C). Shutting off that "trade-*detente*" (or "MBR" -- mutually beneficial reciprocity) will make us more secure internationally? When those collaborating/colluding (with us) even controlling (their own people) despots are overthrown and Islamic extremism goes viral (cyberspace-ically, figuratively, and . . . literally . . .)

Or when the dictators we've so nicely armed (like Saddam) have nothing to lose by turning on our interests? Even on us per se? Turning their people on us? "Go fly . . ."

I interpret any threat that China, Russia, etc. represents as inversely proportionate to our involving them in global economics, trade, labor, etc. Would it really be in the interests of China to turn on us militarily? But if they had nothing to lose . . .. because then they'd be our operant adversary ("enemy", actual, not just currency-level). The mutuality of manufacture and monetary matters would cease. Their assault to seize resources (petro and other) from us (and others) might have to provide their survival.

We shut off "foreign oil" and nothing drastic happens *in the oil realms*? China and India and Russia would so quickly come not only to grasp the whole foreign market, but to become its brokerage houses -- to whomever would pay including No. Korea.

Again as I've reiterated repeatedly more than once (how's that for redundancy?) -- again, though there *may* be illusion regarding the effects ("levels", "degrees") of climate change, any involved exaggeration is really caution. Just in case!! But the illusion of threat, the illusion AS threat, is that our domestic "conventional" resources are so vast that we really don't need to be concerned other than how quickly and prodigiously we can pump and mine their substances and convert them through the alchemy of refinery into . . . cheaper gas and higher petro-profits!!!! . . and pollution.

What a remarkable situation it is that has the "conservative" stance so profligately promoting short-term exploitation for the quick buck. Fuck the generations hence. They'll be bitching about Federal deficits left to encumber them? They'll be far more discomfited by the cold and dark and immobility because we used up, sucked dry, the existential wealth of resources to propel our profits and hi-tech mobile-rampancy. Our "manic-modernicity".

Maybe those in future-shock (and "aw, *shit!* " reactions) will wonder why we didn't put more money (even subsidy) into "renewable" energies and components and infrastructural systems for their implementation as, at least, "collaborating alternatives" with the, thus, much reduced conventional-resource-fuel demands.

. The resources of profit (even "inverse-profit" by lowered prices) are finite.

But he future is not finite There will be children after the children who may still not have to worry about where the means for the heat or light or motion are going to come from. Eventually, though, there will be ongoing generations that will out-live the non-reproducing resources!! Conventional reproduction will outlive conventional production.

But so many would say, "Screw them. What'd they ever do for me?"

So yeah, let's pump it out wherever it is. Let's pipe it from wherever to all over (at least in North America but we'll shut off all those other taps so their economies can collapse if not for China and Russia etc. etc). Yeah, slice off those mountains and burn up that coal. It'll last 'til I'm gone, my kids too, probably. Their kids? Eh? Grand kids? What'd those great-grand kids ever do for me or my kids anyway?

Yeah, let's have cheap gas so we can drive all over the place, run each mouthful of food an average (not median) of 1500 miles, transport carnival prize cartoon figures by the container-full all the way across oceans (this way) and autos and appliances faulty in mere components but crushed or pulverized for shipment all the way across the seas the other way.

Yeah, use up that petro. Don't let it lie around. Ain't makin money in the ground, is it?

Corn!!! Plant more. Takes a lot of fertilizer and pesticides and that takes petro and makes mucho money as the price of corn rises and makes mucho money and the hell with the factor of former food!

Plastic!!!! Let's put people to work making more action figures and plastic fancy shoes to be venture-capitalized as Internet startups and we can fill more and more retail places with plastic and superfluity and indulgence in excess. The clothing discarded overwhelms re-use as clothing.The general merchandise so quick to be redesignated "trash" overwhelms the places to put it now as landfills are reaching capacity.

But you feel that there's malaise. There's foreign interference in our sucking sovereignty. There's entanglements now, and greater military needs . . . now unreduced carbon emissions?? . . .

So let's pump up the petro and profits and pride ourselves in providing paucity for posterity.

That'll relieve the country's malaise???

White bales are white clothes!

www.ingramcontent.com/pod-product-compliance
Lightning Source LLC
Chambersburg PA
CBHW081237180526
45171CB00005B/454
* 9 7 8 1 3 0 0 4 3 7 2 9 1 *